...ISE FOR PAR...

"In *Party of One*, Joy Beth Smith chooses to go where many of us fear (or simply don't want) to tread on the topic of singleness. With raw vulnerability, and unflinching honesty, Joy Beth pushes past easy questions and answers about singleness and relationships. Instead she invites us into her own story and journey, and the conversations many women are having every day. *Party of One* is tender, passionate, and sometimes uncomfortable all at the same time. It's not a book for the fainthearted, or for well-worn platitudes. But I'd also say it's important reading as we listen to, support, invest in, and empower the single members of our community."

—Jo Saxton, speaker, author, chair of 3Dmovements,
and cohost of *Lead Stories* podcast

"Anyone who has signed a True Love Waits pledge (me), written letters to her future husband (also me), or politely nodded along while friends and family gave unsolicited dating advice (again, me) will be nodding and laughing along to Joy Beth's honest account of the confusing experience that so often is Christian singleness. What Joy Beth offers readers is the permission and freedom to make the most of singleness, defining it not by what it lacks but by what promise it holds. This book is a gift to the church and to readers from all walks of life."

—Katelyn Beaty, author of *A Woman's Place*
and *Christianity Today* editor at large

"Joy Beth Smith's voice—honest, fearless, funny, and wise—is exactly what we need in the conversation about Christian singleness. Her book will bring healing to a church culture that desperately needs it, and offers a healthy, positive vision of what singleness can look like for faithful Christians. An essential read."

—Gina Dalfonzo, author of *One by One*

"I experienced *Party of One* as one long *exhale*. Finally comes a book that speaks the language of both soul and sexuality without any squeamishness. Finally comes a book that is both devout and devoid of the weird stodginess religious people have about their bodies under the guise of 'reverence.' If the gospel teaches us anything, it's that we don't have to choose between humanity and divinity. In that same Christian spirit, *Party of One* demonstrates that we don't have to choose between funny and fierce, boldness and tenderness, or laughter and tears. Somewhere at the intersection of Hildegard of Bingen and Tina Fey, God gave us Joy Beth Smith."

—Jonathan Martin, author of *How to Survive a Shipwreck* and *Prototype*

"'Singleness isn't a season of preparation for something better.' Amen. Today is the gift, and Jesus is the prize. The church is in dire need of a more robust theology and practice when it comes to singleness and Joy Beth leads the way with humor and wisdom that cut through the fluff. This isn't one of those 'what to do while you're waiting for a husband' kind of books, so pick it up and be encouraged."

—Hayley Morgan, coauthor of the bestselling book *Wild and Free*

"This is the book I wish I would have read as a single woman. Joy Beth speaks with clarity, compassion, wit, and frankness about so many of the unique struggles and triumphs of navigating singleness in our current culture. She doesn't shy away from difficult topics and alternatively offers her readers the warm, understanding hug and the kick in the pants they might need. This is a must-read for both singles and married folks who want to put singleness in a proper, biblical perspective. I cannot recommend it enough."

—Jasmine Holmes, author and creator of *Not a Mommy Blog*

"*Party of One* frees us from the nest of lies we encounter as single adults in Christianity. Joy Beth untangles the beliefs that insist prolonged singleness is a result of sin, singles are lacking in wisdom, and sexuality is a simple matter. Christians have—for too long—needed someone to wade into the complexity of these issues, without flinching, and to lead us through it. Joy Beth has done just that with stirring eloquence and reassuring bravery."

—Paul Maxwell, author of *When Your Twenties Are Darker Than You Expected*

"Joy Beth Smith writes a timeless anthem for the ones often feeling singled out by singleness. Her prose is refreshing and kind, like an old friend sitting down with you for a cup of tea. A truth-teller who isn't afraid to talk about the stuff we so often shove into the corner, Joy Beth gives the greatest gift a writer can give their reader: a series of honest 'me too' moments that empower and push us all—single, dating, married—to be better."

—Hannah Brencher, author of *Come Matter Here*

"This book is a triumph of truth and empathy for those living the single life and those who are long hitched! After being married twenty-five years, reading *Party of One* out loud to each other was one of the most enjoyable ways to spend our evenings. It stirred up our desire to reclaim those deep, foundational lessons God began in our own lives while we were single, honoring the meaningful, whole, and beautiful lives we each have. Everyone, regardless of marital status, should read Joy Beth's welcoming, witty, and provocative work."

—Stephan and Belinda Bauman, authors and speakers

"I'm a married Puerto Rican pastor who absolutely loved this book. I was challenged and inspired by Joy Beth's journey. Her wit and faith are a winning combination. You will read, cry, laugh, cringe, and be challenged to truly know yourself (while being inspired to love whatever wild ride God has you on). And as a married Puerto Rican pastor who used to preach a lot of the things Joy Beth calls out in her book, I can only say: I'm so sorry! While it may be written to singles, this is a book every pastor, parent, church leader, and married friend needs to read."

—Carlos Rodríguez, founder of Happy Sonship
and author of *Drop the Stones*

"The stories and research behind *Party of One* provide a solid, relatable framework for exploring the questions of longing and lament as well as the beauty and freedom of single life. Whether you're just entering the college dating scene or you've rocked it solo for decades, you're going to want your own copy of this book for all the 'me too's you'll want to write in the margins. Grab a copy and a pen, because the party is just getting started."

—Jenna, 29, assistant editor

"For an older, single woman like myself, reading *Party of One* is like being invited into a conversation your heart longs for, but rarely finds. Stuff gets real with an unapologetic flair that makes you want to join in the discussion, despite the hesitation anyone feels when talking about typically taboo subjects. No one talks about these topics because we are afraid of exposure, and yet we are not meant to live life in the shallow end. We are called to community, one that goes deep, and that is what this book encourages us to do—come find your place at the table, celebrate it, and know that you are not alone."

—Christina, 36, program director

"This book is everything. I'm a pretty tough critic and typically hate Christian women's self-improvement and encouragement books because I feel like they lack a sense of honesty and understanding that God isn't a vending machine, but this was everything I needed and more."

—Meghan, 24, missionary

"This book is a gift for those of us who oftentimes feel like we are navigating the single life alone, but it's also a gift for the Church at large. Everyone wins when the body of Christ embraces and celebrates her single members—doubts, dreams, and all!"

—Kendall, 27, baker and writer

"*Party of One* unveils the reality and struggles of being a single woman in a way that is greatly needed in the church. Joy Beth covers all the bases by addressing the language and treatment that unmarried adults can be exposed to, and she's not afraid to bring it home with a no-holds-barred discussion on sex and singleness. While *Party of One* is written for single ladies, it's relevant for all that desire to build community."

—Meghan, 33, childcare worker

"*Party of One* reads like a conversation with your best friend at a favorite coffee shop. Joy Beth's writing invites you to the table with hilarious confessions of her personal experiences that make you feel truly welcomed. Her enthusiasm cheers you on to push past your frustrations and disappointments so that you can begin to celebrate and enjoy the life you have, however unexpected it may be."

—Tory, 29, artist

"In these pages, I found my own beliefs, fears, questions, longings, struggles, resolve, and even a few new perspectives I hadn't considered before, looking back at me. In a church culture that values marriage, but overlooks singleness (even unintentionally), *Party of One* is a welcome friendship that offers a respite from the loneliness. The book has in mind single women as its primary audience, but I hope pastors and other church leaders everywhere will read it to learn how to better shepherd their singles."

—Lucy, 34, freelance editor

"Reading *Party of One* was like finally, for the first time in my life, having a conversation with someone who truly understands. This book is full of things I never see discussed openly, but that we're desperately in need of. There are so many tender bits inside me from being single for so long, and Joy Beth is the friend I needed—someone who doesn't mince words when she shares her story, is willfully vulnerable, and makes you whisper 'yes, yes, this' over your cup of coffee as she points to the only marriage any of us were ever guaranteed."

—Jenn, 35, web developer

"This book will have you turning the pages, laughing, and saying 'Yes, queen!' in agreement. It captures the essence of dating in today's world. All the questions you've had and thought you were alone with are now on the table with us fabulous and single women. So, let's talk."

—Lauryn, 28, nanny

"After reading *Party of One*, I couldn't help but wonder if Joy Beth had been creeping on my text messages like some faceless government agent to pull material for her book. Her words resonated soundly through my entire being, giving a broader voice to so many thoughts and beliefs I've developed as I tried desperately to improve myself to better my chances, then to somehow learn to love myself when that failed, and finally as I began to accept myself, warts and all. She speaks with a humor, grace, and frankness that is infectious and eases the shock of some topics that have been wrongly tabooed for millennia."

—Maggie, 23, student

PARTY of One

TRUTH, LONGING, AND
THE SUBTLE ART OF SINGLENESS

JOY BETH SMITH

NELSON
BOOKS

An Imprint of Thomas Nelson

Published in Nashville, Tennessee, by Nelson Books, an imprint of Thomas Nelson. Nelson Books and Thomas Nelson are registered trademarks of HarperCollins Christian Publishing, Inc.

Published in association with the literary agency D.C. Jacobson & Associates, LLC, an Author Management Company, www.dcjacobson.com.

Thomas Nelson titles may be purchased in bulk for educational, business, fundraising, or sales promotional use. For information, please e-mail SpecialMarkets@ThomasNelson.com.

ISBN 978-0-7180-94096 (eBook)

Library of Congress Cataloging-in-Publication Data

ISBN 978-0-7180-94058
Names: Smith, Joy Beth, 1988- author.
Title: Party of one : truth, longing, and the subtle art of singleness / Joy Beth Smith.
Description: Nashville : Thomas Nelson, 2018. | Includes bibliographical references.
Identifiers: LCCN 2017033353 | ISBN 9780718094058
Subjects: LCSH: Christian women--Religious life. | Sex--Religious aspects--Christianity. | Single people--Sexual behavior. | Christian women--Sexual behavior. | Single people--Religious life.
Classification: LCC BV4527 .S629 2018 | DDC 248.8/432--dc23 LC record available at https://lccn.loc.gov/2017033353

Printed in the United States of America

18 19 20 21 22 LSC 10 9 8 7 6 5 4 3 2 1

Dedicated to all the amazing women I've met, and those I haven't, who inspire me with their wild and precious lives. Thank you.

CONTENTS

CONTENTS

FOREWORD

I am tired of writing about single life.

There. I said it.

I've carried the moniker "The Single Woman" for going on a decade now, and sometimes I think I've said absolutely everything there is to say about single life. Three books, hundreds of blogs, and thousands of tweets later, I've definitely contributed more than my two cents to the conversation.

But here's the thing. Three books, hundreds of blogs, and thousands of tweets later . . . there's still not much of a conversation happening.

The church and singleness: Why is it rather like oil and water? Like Chick-fil-A and Sundays? Like me and kale? Why do the two just seem to not fit together no matter how desperately we might want them to?

The church, and Christianity as a whole, doesn't seem to quite know what to do with us singletons. There seems to be a great deal of fear and hesitation and uncertainty and even disinterest in addressing some of the great, big, difficult issues that single believers contend with every single day.

I'm happy to tell you, dear friends, that this book doesn't hold one single ounce of that fear or hesitation. It is bold and strong and unapologetic. Unflinching, even. Much like its author, Joy Beth Smith. Joy Beth doesn't back down from those hard conversations that need to be happening, not just in our churches but in our small groups, our social circles, our relationships.

I've never met Joy Beth in person. As is the modern way of making connections and forming friendships, we connected online a few years ago when she edited a piece I wrote for *Today's Christian Woman*. At some point along the way, I started following her personal Twitter page. And it was like a breath of fresh air. Her perspectives on life and love and faith and singleness are real and raw and relatable and funny. When you read her work, you feel like you're chatting with an old friend.

An old friend who isn't afraid to address some *really* tough topics as it relates to singleness, dating, and marriage. Joy Beth touches on some issues I haven't even been brave enough to tackle in nearly a decade of narrating the single journey! Prepare to be uncomfortable at times. Prepare to be challenged at times. You might want to even prepare to blush at times. This isn't just another "polite Christian book." But isn't that the very essence of what this whole faith and life journey should be about? Facing the awkwardness and the discomfort and the uncertainty and pressing through to see what's on the other side?

Press through, friends, to the other side. It's a journey

you won't regret. And along the way, you might find more than a real, authentic, brave conversation about single life. You might just find yourself.

—Mandy Hale, creator of The Single Woman™ and *New York Times* bestselling author

PART I

UNFULFILLED PROMISES

1

GOD DOESN'T OWE
YOU A HUSBAND

I had to pause, yet again, to stretch out my fingers. I could type for hours a day, yet writing with even my best pens for more than fifteen minutes left my hand cramped. But I had to keep going—I had to finish the letter. I pushed through the pain, using it to fuel my last words, words full of passion and love and promises of a future together. With a flourish, I signed the bottom of the page, "Love you always, Your Wife."

I folded the letter carefully and slipped it inside an envelope scented with my favorite perfume (a lovely floral number that *Glamour* told me most men prefer in a blind smell test). I quickly scrawled "To My Husband" on the front as I said a little prayer and slid it into the large hatbox where it rested next to hundreds of its siblings.

I had written a letter to my future husband at least once

a month for the past fifteen years. These letters, if compiled and published, could act as one of the most prolific (or most embarrassing) coming-of-age missives in recent history. They're full of heartbreak and longing, questions of faith, and milestones in my academic life and career. In the course of writing these letters, I shopped for a prom dress, graduated high school, excelled at college, changed my major (three times), and then finally attended grad school. They followed me through painful years of unrequited love and crushes that lived up to their name. I wrote about horrible dates and dreams of what was to come. But in recent months these letters had grown increasingly skeptical. Not of the Lord delivering a husband, as one might assume. Rather, the letters seemed to be in the middle of an existential crisis, questioning their own purpose and existence.

I had spent untold hours recording the details of my existence for a man who, statistically speaking, probably wouldn't enjoy the stream-of-conscious minutia of a sixteen-year-old cheerleader. But I had read about this idea in a book, how the wife wrote letters to her husband and then gave them to him on their wedding day, and they both cried. While the sentiment is indeed very romantic, I can't imagine many men really enjoying the experience of reading hundreds of repetitive letters peppered with the egregious misspellings, poor reasoning, and spotty theology of youth. I imagine marrying a man who would much prefer a pocket watch or organic beard oil as a wedding present.

One day, tired of my own antics in preparation for the husband I had yet to meet, I burned the letters. All of them. I took my lavender-scented candle and lit the edge of one envelope on fire. Then, after nearly burning my hand while caught up in my own melodrama, I dropped it into a metal trash can and began the process again—over and over until all my words were nothing more than ash. Even as I was in the process of burning the last of the letters, I concocted some kind of poetic beauty from the ashes, imagining what phoenix may arise next.

I've yet to see the phoenix, but I did realize that day how much time I spent pining for more than what I had—for what I liked to think was the inevitable but in reality is not. Here's the thing: Marriage is not inevitable. Motherhood is not inevitable. And yet, at any given family gathering, I hear this phrase at least once: "God's got such a wonderful husband in store for you. Just wait. Keep being faithful."

In reality, God has promised me many, many things: joy, intimacy with him, comfort, the presence of the Holy Spirit, and eternal life, just to name a few. But I'll never find the promise of a husband, of a beautiful, fulfilling marriage, tucked away in the back of James or even alluded to in Psalms. As much as I long for this thing—this good, beautiful thing—I am not entitled to it. God never promises me a God-fearing husband, satisfaction guaranteed.

The problem is, I've believed this unscriptural promise for years. And if we're being honest, we all have to some extent. So many lies about singleness are ingrained in our religious culture—even embedded in the very infrastructure of the church. Some are easy to spot, while others are so tightly woven in that it feels impossible to find a way around them. But if we are to live the full lives God has given us, we can't simply follow along with what we've been told. We need to dig deep into Scripture and find the truth, distinguishing between what is biblical and what is merely cultural—or even flat-out wrong.

The first lie we should eliminate, as I mentioned earlier, is the way we assume marriage is coming for us. For the better part of my life I felt that it was almost owed to me. But marriage, like so many other parts of life, is a gift that God has the right to withhold, should he so desire. I deeply believe that the Lord is good, that he is faithful and sovereign. Yet somehow I have to reconcile this understanding with the facts: some women will spend their lives desperately wanting a husband only to never receive one.

This is not an easy truth to face. It reminds me of that portion of 2 Samuel 6 where God kills Uzzah for trying to steady the ark of the covenant after an ox stumbles. God struck him dead. I can't understand that. It's hard for me. Like it's hard for me to know that marriage is a good thing— especially a marriage that honors God through two people growing to be more like him—but he doesn't always give us all the good things, even when we *really, really* want them.

Honestly, it's crushing to live under the constant weight of unmet desires. It's hard to long for something you have little to no control over actually obtaining. It's hard to see people in happy marriages. It's hard to sit alone in your apartment on Thanksgiving wishing you had rolls to burn or a pie to botch and a husband to console you afterward.

Even though I'm no longer spending my evenings writing letters to a faceless figment of my imagination who strongly resembles a bearded Clark Kent, I'll often find myself daydreaming of a husband. That's silly and embarrassing to admit, but it's true. It's usually in the mundane moments when I feel the absence of a husband most profoundly. On my drive home from work when I want to pop into a store and pick up a surprise treat for dessert, just because I know it's his favorite. During those extra-long weekends as I'm choosing an outfit, trying to remember which blue shirt it was that he complimented. As I sit in church and feel a physical ache in my hands from where I want to be holding his. But I'm learning that indulging these daydreams is fuel for discontentment, and I can't afford that right now. There is so much life God has given me to live, with or without a husband, and I can't waste it sitting in my disappointments. In fact, I refuse to.

Instead, I want to drink deeply of life and let go of all the rest. And I want to do it with my sisters, bringing community to those who feel isolated, hope to those who feel desperate, and truth to those who feel deceived. Together, I hope we can excavate the harmful assumptions that have permeated the church for far too long, rooting them out and planting truth in their place.

MAKING ROOM AT THE TABLE

Tables are significant to me. Because I'm an extreme extrovert, they represent the place where I recharge, where I find people I can connect with, where food gets cold because we can't stop talking or laughing long enough to shovel it in. Tables are for community building and healing. So when I set out to write this book, I wanted to do so in the context of this community. I had my own experiences with being a Christian single, but I wanted to go beyond that and seek out others with different perspectives to contribute. I did many one-on-one interviews, but the shared communal experience felt more significant. I thought something important would happen in gathering women around a table.

Before I even got the contract for this book deal, when the idea was still in the proposal stage, I gathered a group of ten women in Chicago, where I lived. Each of us nursed a cup of coffee, tea, or, for those adventurous ones, mint hot chocolate. Most of us were strangers—even I had only met three of the women previously. And in coming together in a safe place, with drinks and food and laughter ringing around the rafters, we had a little taste of heaven on earth. Something important *did* happen.

Over the course of three hours, we laughed and cried. We acted as intercessors and confessors. We received one another's heartaches with weight and grace. And then we left, and most of us haven't seen one another since. But many of us (thanks to social media) remain deeply connected, forged by a bond of mutual respect and appreciation that comes from having gone to war together. We've fought through something significant, and now we're braver and better for it.

We realized that at the table, truth comes out. Ultimately, we'd come together for one purpose: we wanted to talk about singleness. How it's so hard. Why it's so difficult. How we're coping. What we're doing. How we're struggling.

Because honestly, if you're single, you're probably struggling in some way. You might be perfectly well-adjusted and incredibly content and utterly at peace with your situation, but you're still struggling. Maybe you struggle to bear the hopes that family or well-meaning small-group members place on you, that heavy mantle of the expectation of marriage. Maybe it's that you feel called to be a wife and a mom, and now you're in a place where you're hopelessly helpless to make it happen. Or maybe you feel isolated in your singleness, feeling as if you're the only one who's actually *not okay.*

That's what I wanted these women to know—that it's okay not to be okay. That I'm not okay. And that only by having frank conversations can we open up to one another, share one another's burdens, stories, wounds, and wisdom, and begin to heal. A salve comes from friendship and shared experiences that is sweet and powerful.

So we gathered around a table, these women and I, and we talked. Though we'd just met, that didn't hinder the conversation in the least; if anything, it was freeing. What would you say about your fears and insecurities to a group of women if you never had to see them again—if you knew that they experienced the same things?

THE REDEFINING NATURE OF MARRIAGE

As I opened the discussion by recalling the all-too-common, painful practice of people promising a husband is in store for me, Patty, a thirtysomething public school teacher, interjected: "What store? Where can I find it? I'll go shopping! Do they have a Black Friday sale? Two for one?"

We all laughed, but the truth of her words hit me. There is no store. And no one can claim what's "in store" for me, as if there's some catalog and they have an advance copy. As Patty went on to explain, when people say this, when they assure us of a future that is unassurable, "It hurts. Because if these are people who love me, they know that I'm waiting for whatever God has for me—no matter what that is. But the truth is that we don't know what's in store; none of us does."

The worst part comes when they're so sure of this conviction that God must have a husband in store that they decide to go shopping for you. Oh, how quickly the marrieds forget what it's like to be single. They try to pair you off with any man who has all his teeth and a functioning liver, but the reality is that only a year ago you were in a small group with that well-meaning couple when they were both single, and they never would have tried to get you to go out with Trevor, the accountant with gingivitis and a wandering eye. But marriage happens, and relationship dynamics change. And suddenly marriage is supposed to happen for all the single people as well, so the playing field can be leveled once again (and so their relationships will be easier to manage and understand, even if it means you dating Trevor).

This well-intentioned act conveys a different message. When people try to pair us up, two by two, and shove us in the ark of the marrieds, it feels as though we're being pawned off, as if we're compromising the potential of what God has for us. Instead of being excited for our lives and willing to sit with us in our singleness, they're anxious for this season to end. In reality, our goals should be the same: to honor

God, in singleness and in marriage. And very rarely does that look like spending every Friday night rotating through a panel of dates who make us question our education system and the increasing neglect of cologne. At the end of the day, I want my people to want the glory of God in my life more than they want me to be married. But is that actually what's playing out in conversations and activities?

People offer placating words, and often they come from a good place, but every once in a while they're simply knee-jerk responses. Perhaps, for instance, in a moment of weakness, after you've gotten your car stuck on yet another snowdrift and have to wait for AAA to come tow you out while you battle hypothermia, you finally get up the courage to voice one of your deepest fears to some close friends: "What if I never meet someone?"

And then someone responds too quickly, almost flippantly, "Oh, you'll get married."

"But that is so presumptuous," Katelyn Beaty, author of *A Woman's Place*, said at a roundtable. "I know a ton of wonderful women you would have said that to ten years ago, and they're still not married. I think it's some naiveté speaking: 'This was my experience, I got married at twenty-six, so this will happen for you.' There's good intention there, but it's claiming to know something that they can't possibly know. And it's not actually helpful."

As the girls and I rattled on about our experiences of people using this barb almost as a weapon against our doubts of the future, Doni, a thirty-seven-year-old marketing guru, brought us back to reality, back to hope. "I think we should ground this discussion in some truth," she said, and we all prepared ourselves, because anyone who dresses so stylishly and has such great hair must have something important to say. "We can hope in marriage, because it is promised, but it's not an earthly one. We are part of the bride; our bridegroom awaits, and he has gone to make a better place and to prepare a home for us.

"I think it's beautiful that we can hold to this idea of marriage and oneness for all eternity—it's just not the limited scope of one man and one woman. It's us, the bride, and the King of kings and Lord of lords. We will be married one day, just maybe not in the earthly sense."

And you know what? Doni's right. She's more right than we can ever imagine. There is a good man in store for me—the best man who ever walked this earth, in fact. I have a marriage in store. I have a union and oneness waiting for me. *That* is the truth on which I should be basing my assumptions, hopes, and dreams. The earthly marriage? That may come (and I hope and pray that it does). But the eternal marriage of the church and the Bridegroom? That's a ceremony you're all invited to, so save the date.

YES, THE STRUGGLE *IS* REAL

We all know that Genesis opens with God creating Adam. Remember how Adam lost a rib and gained a wife? As much as we know and feel that it's not good for man to be alone, we might not be an Eve with an Adam. We might be an Esther with a Mordecai. A Hannah with a Samuel. A Jesus with a John. A Paul with a Timothy. You weren't meant to fight through this life alone, to do battle by yourself—but the companion promised to you won't necessarily wear a platinum wedding band and fold towels the wrong way.

Or, you know what? He just might.

I think that's the hardest part about being single: never knowing when this time will end. Every day could be the day your life changes. Every unmarried man you meet could be the man you spend the rest of your life with. Every message you get on the sketchy dating site could be the message that starts a conversation that leads to a meeting that ends at an altar. Or you could think this way every single day for ten years, but none of these things happen. Men come and go, messages are sent with no reply, and day by day, your singleness grows into a thing that feels cumbersome and heavy and threatening.

You never know when it's going to end—*if* it's going to end—and in the midst of this uncertainty, in the midst of this questioning and pain, you're somehow supposed to trust God implicitly. To be proactive but not overactive. To help the Lord's plan along but not overtake it. To glean the fields and lie on the threshing floor but not (Facebook) stalk your Boaz. These are hazy lines at best.

And this is exactly why we have to crush this lie. It's *hard* to live in this tension of desperately wanting something and never knowing when or if it will come. We need to actively cling to promises that *are* in Scripture: promises that God will never leave us, promises of his control in all things, promises of his goodness, promises that the trials of this world pale in comparison to the glory of what is to come. These are sure things.

A husband is not a sure thing.

We can't continue to put prophecies in the Lord's mouth and call it comfort. We can't *believe* these promises and call them sound theology. Somehow there's middle ground here of seeing the sanctity of marriage, hoping for that end, believing God to be good, yet not placing all our hopes on God delivering a man.

God giving you a husband does not prove his goodness— marriage isn't even inherently good. But God is good, always. He is good in your singleness. He is good in your foolishness when you make stupid decisions because of singleness. And if you're in this same place ten years from now, he will still be good. But when God's goodness becomes dependent on his delivery, you have perverted the true gospel into nothing more than a prosperity message.

In discussing this idea of God's goodness, Paige Benton Brown wrote, "It is a cosmic impossibility for God to shortchange any of his children. . . . I am not single because I am too unstable to possibly deserve a husband, nor because I am too spiritually mature to possibly need one. I am single because God is so abundantly good to me, because this is his best for me."[1] If I'm single today, it is because God is good to me, so good that he loves me enough to save me from less than his best—and for whatever reason, that's marriage. I am a have—not a have-not.

Many of the well-intentioned people in our lives act as Peter did in Matthew 16. As Jesus was about to be taken away, he told the disciples he was about to die. And sweet Peter cried out, "Far be it from you, Lord! This shall never happen to you."

What a great comfort he must have thought that affirmation would be to the Lord. But instead Jesus responded with my favorite response whenever anyone offers me yet another cookie and I'm trying to fit into yet another bridesmaid's dress: "Get behind me, Satan!"[2]

Just because we have seemingly encouraging or positive things to say to someone doesn't make them biblical or even good or true.

So let's find the good, the true, and the beautiful, and let's leave the rest.

2

SINGLENESS ISN'T SEASONAL

*For everything there is a season, and a
time for every matter under heaven.*

ECCLESIASTES 3:1

I used to hate this verse. There are lots of verses in the Bible
that make me uncomfortable or irritated, and this used to
be one of them. It probably has less to do with the Bible and
more to do with the fact that this passage feeds one of the
most annoying clichés unmarried people hear all the time:
singleness is for a season.

It seems that whenever I'm feeling especially sad or
desperate or sure I'll never be married to a bug-killing, tea-
drinking son of a gun, someone, with the best of intentions,
offers this verse as comfort. Most of the time when people

use this phrase, they're trying to encourage me that this time spent wandering the aisles of the local grocery store at nine o'clock on a Friday night is limited. Because, like all difficult things, this too shall pass. This season will *definitely* come to an end. There are better things still to come! So throw on an extra-thick scarf, bow your head into the wind, and muscle through.

If you don't glean anything else from this chapter, even this book, I hope this sinks straight into your soul: singleness is not simply a season to be weathered, a waiting room, or a holding cell. It's not temporal by design, and it doesn't exist only to usher you into something greater. Singleness is a valid life stage, one in which you can experience as much joy, spiritual growth, and fulfillment as any married person.

When we treat singleness like an elevator ride, a necessary interlude to a desired destination, we reduce our contributions, relationships, and ministries to elevator music and idle chitchat with strangers while we wait for the floors to zoom past. What a waste. This stage of your life, even if it lasts for your entire life, is something so much greater than a funnel to marriage.

This is where I'd like to redirect us to a mostly forgotten passage in the Bible. It sits in one of the popular books, but I haven't heard this bit preached from the pulpit lately. In 1 Corinthians 7:8–9, the apostle Paul said, "To the unmarried and the widows I say that it is good for them to remain single, as I am. But if they cannot exercise self-control, they should marry. For it is better to marry than to burn with passion."

At the time Paul wrote these words, he was speaking to

people who, rather than constantly looking to get past a season of singleness, were actually trying to stay single—they were emulating Paul—and in doing so, many were sinning sexually. Paul was basically acknowledging that while singleness is enjoyable, even preferable, it's not worth staying single if it's causing someone to sin.

Nowadays, it seems that the default, the expected, is marriage; and I need the constant reminder to not allow my chasing after marriage to cause me to sin. This flip from the way Paul viewed singleness and marriage is fascinating. Get this: singleness was once the ideal, hence the legacy of monks and nuns who stay celibate in order to devote their lives to Christ. Singleness wasn't simply a short season of life that Christians tolerated before they could reach the pinnacle of being (a.k.a. marriage).

The problem with viewing singleness as a season is that we relegate our time here to something to be endured, not celebrated. It becomes like the depths of winter in Chicago when everyone avoids eye contact, rushes home from work, and disables their dating accounts. (True story: One winter I found five different profiles from men who said they wouldn't be active from December to March, but they'd be happy to grab coffee after that. Hibernation seriously hurt my dating game, because I can rock a cute sweater dress, scarf, and boots.)

We all seem to be hunkering down and waiting for that next season to start. But the thing is, friends, singleness is not a season with a guaranteed end in this life. And we can't spend our days trying to wait it out, constantly looking for what we hope is coming next. Does that mean that while sitting in the blustery days of fall it's wrong of me to think wistfully of snow and hot chocolate and ugly sweaters? No, I don't believe so—not at first anyway. Longing for winter, for the next thing, becomes a problem only when we're unable to then enjoy and fully live in the present.

A large part of the struggle to steward our singleness well rather than reducing it to a blip on the radar seems to be in the church's approach. Shurti, a thirty-four-year-old dentist from our Nashville roundtable, discussed the church's inability to encourage and engage single people: "No one knows how to minister to singles. No one affirms that this phase of life is okay." When leaders in our lives don't understand the struggles of being single, they often default to pushing us through to a stage they do understand. Shurti continued, "A lot of pastors got married in their early twenties, so they have no idea how to be single and thirty-four. But why isn't there a singles ministry? Why isn't someone saying 'This is what it's like to walk as a single woman'? It's a hole that the church doesn't know how to fill."

More often than not, even if your church has a singles ministry, it ends up feeling less like an opportunity for growth and discipleship and more like an elaborate dating game, one that exists solely to pair you up and marry you off. If the church believed singleness could be more than simply a season to be tolerated, they'd be investing in resources that backed that up. But instead, everything from the language on the bulletin down to the name of the groups seems designed to reinforce the idea that this time is supposed to be temporary. And it starts to feel as though your status in the church is defined by your relationship status on

Facebook. Instead of asking about your job, your spiritual struggles, or even your progress in your boxing class, people inquire constantly about your love life. And, at least in my case, the more uncomfortable other people seem to be with my singleness, the more uncomfortable I am with it.

Heather, a forty-one-year-old single mom, shared her experience: "Even when pastors do pray for you, they pray for your husband to come. It's like singleness is a waiting room, like what I have isn't enough."

Friends, this is simply not true! Let's not bow to this cultural idea that singleness doesn't cut it as a way of life, because until we dispel this notion from our minds, we can't start learning what it means to be satisfied in the lives we've been given.

NOT ONE BUT MANY

Rather than considering singleness as a season in itself, it's more worthwhile to acknowledge the many different seasons that exist within it. If the only thing that remains constant in your life is that you get to hog the covers without feeling guilty, undoubtedly you will still experience great mountains and valleys, victories and defeats. Though others may tend to infantilize you, and their view of you may remain stagnant because of your unmarried state, we ladies know the truth—the single life has many stages.

From my own experience, there's been the single-in-college stage where I was content to walk to a boy's dorm every night and talk to him at his window (I promise, it was a cool thing to do since girls weren't allowed inside), knowing he'd never like me but hoping he'd change his mind. My single-in-grad-school phase looked a bit different. I was overwhelmed with my thesis, content with my life, and excited for my future. Being alone didn't feel like much of a burden when I was living with my best friends and experiencing the joy of teaching at a collegiate level. Single-and-in-the-workforce, now that required a lot from me. Spending days in a cubicle, only to come home to an empty apartment and huge decisions that had to be made with only me to make them. All of it felt overwhelmingly lonely. But single-and-almost-thirty is better. I'm adjusting to being alone without feeling as lonely, and I'm learning how to balance my longing for marriage with the reality of my situation.

My experience with singleness may hardly resemble yours, and my singleness now may be far removed from my singleness in another decade, so let's be gracious to ourselves and instill value into the lives we're living by using language that honors our different experiences.

In talking about this with others, I've found one way of being mindful of this kind of grace is drawing a parallel between infertility and singleness. It's not a perfect comparison, and I by no means want to minimize the unique struggle of each, but I do think there's something to be learned from looking at the two side by side.

When a woman is facing infertility, her desire for a child is seen as beautiful, natural, and good. We encourage different methods of treating the infertility, everything from drinking herbal teas to rubbing oak bark on one's belly. If a woman has struggled for years with infertility, we mourn the children who might have been and all the lost hopes and dreams with her. And all the while, we make promises we know we have no power to keep: *The Lord will give you children. I got pregnant after five years of trying, so I know that'll happen to you as well.*

Perhaps the Lord will give this couple children years from now, or perhaps he won't. Who are we to analyze God's intentions?

In the same way, the desire singles experience for marriage is beautiful, natural, and good. And too often people encourage ways to "treat" the singleness by offering their best advice on how and where to find a mate, how to push them from one season to the next. And if those tips prove fruitless, they double down on the promises: *This is just a season you have to go through. Keep being faithful in searching, and God will be faithful in providing.*

Infertility and singleness both contain innumerable types of experiences, and we can't oversimplify them by offering promises that may not be true—promises that, if we're honest, point back to a mind-set that undervalues the life stage the person is struggling to live out well. We don't like messy, and we don't like pain. It's so much harder to just sit with the woman who's been trying for four years to have kids or the single woman who longs for marriage but, despite her best efforts, remains single. But empathy, and sitting in that pain, naming it, is far more valuable than false comfort and clichéd advice. Only in truly acknowledging the value of each life, of each unique path that God is mapping out, can we come to understand what it means to embrace life and live it well.

PAUL SAID IT WAS GOOD, Y'ALL

If these days and weeks and years of singleness aren't only meant to lay the groundwork for the next season to come and if this stage doesn't have a guaranteed end date, like the first day of winter, then how can we really embrace Paul's idea that it's better to be single? How do we shove aside the voice that tells us to hold on and wait for the upgrade that's coming and instead lean into what we have now?

"I like Paul. He's awesome." Sabrina, a thirty-two-year-old business owner and generally amazing person, was the first in our Nashville roundtable to try and tackle the passage from 1 Corinthians. "He was so focused, and that's why he said what he did. Paul was obsessed with being single and doing him. That's great for Paul, and there are still people like that. But that doesn't make it a mandate for us to be single. We keep going back to this verse because he was the only one in the Bible talking about it."

With so little instruction given directly to single people, it's hard to build a robust theology of singleness. In a lot of ways, that would be the same as a robust theology of Christian living, which is basically what Paul's getting at here.

When I look at the passage, I hear Paul saying, "Look, there's good work to be done right now. And you can do a lot more of that if you're not swooning and falling in love and changing diapers. But if your flesh is driving you to marriage because you need to have sex, go ahead and get married, but know that you'll accomplish less" (JBSV, Joy Beth Standard Version). This feels very logical and straightforward, and I like that. Instead of portraying singleness as a disease in need of a cure, for Paul, singleness was the functioning ideal. And if there is a "disease," it's lust, for which marriage can be the cure.

Jaycelyn, a physician at a children's hospital, saw this passage as one loaded with implied expectations: "People use that verse as a weapon to say, 'If you're single, you should be doing these things. You should be going overseas, or you're not doing it right. You should be working in the children's ministry.' They tell me how to spend my time, my singleness, and no one has the right to do that. I've been criticized for pursuing my career, and people basically say, 'How dare you spend all this time on school and work when you could be serving the church.' But I'm serving sick children, and that's pretty important too."

This is one of my biggest pet peeves with our current message surrounding singleness in the church: singleness is only preferable or equal to marriage when we pull a Mother Teresa and dedicate our whole lives to serving God—or, more accurately, serving God in a visible and public way that other people acknowledge. Singleness that's spent investing in a career (even one you may feel called to) is secondary to babysitting for Mom's Night Out or arriving early to set up for service. But what if God has different plans for some of us than being Mother Teresa Jr. or spending that Friday night babysitting? The church needs to decide if singleness is as beneficial as Paul said it is, and if it is, it should probably be celebrated instead of fixed. Rather than focusing on ushering us out of this season or distracting us from what God is calling us to do in our singleness, we need our church community to figure out a way to come alongside us in our careers and communities and support us in our singleness.

HAND ME MY SASH

Until a few years ago, I'd never really watched a parade, but one Thanksgiving, as I was spending time with a wonderful mentor and mother figure, we got comfy on her couch and sighed happily as the floats edged their way across the screen. The costumes were over the top, gaudy, and covered in sequins, exactly what I'll wear one day if I'm ever in a parade. There were choreographed dances with batons and ribbons, and marching bands flown in from around the country. Happiness and exuberance fell like snowflakes, coating the whole thing in rosy hope.

This, my friends, is what the single life is meant to be. Was the whole purpose of that parade to get from point A to point B as quickly and efficiently as possible? Absolutely not. The purpose of that parade was to play music at deafening levels, to pass out fifteen tons of candy, and to prove that middle-aged dancers can still do the splits on moving floats.

How boring it would be if everyone left their glitter and tutus at home and ran from First Street all the way to the corner of Market and Main. People do that—it's called a race. And your success is only measured by how fast you make it to the finish line. Those who don't finish are either gravely injured or worthy of our deepest pity. We have to stop treating the single life like it's a race to the altar. I'm ready for my parade. I'm ready to trade in my sneakers for a tiara and a sash as I do a princess wave from atop a float. I'm tired of racing toward an invisible finish line that keeps moving farther away the closer I get. I'm tired of staring enviously at the girls who are passing me (and all the while pushing aside my thoughts of tripping them). I'm tired of placing all my hopes and dreams on crossing a finish line that may never come.

I want to enjoy the journey. I want to take pride in the parade that is my life. One of my best friends, Meghan, is amazing at this. She is totally happy riding in the parade. She wants to be married, but this girl *carpes* the dang *diem* every day. She loves her career and has even recently gone back to school. She visits friends who need help with their multiple babies. She sends me presents just because. She invests in her church. She rides that float and waves to the crowd and throws candy at the kids. And all the while, her life reminds me that in this time there is purpose and joy. I want to learn to live more like that.

GOOGLE MAPS WON'T HELP YOU HERE

The blessed reality behind Paul's words is that singleness isn't for the outcast, isolated, or irredeemable. Singleness is a valid path to choose, and if you are one of those amazing women who are happy in their singleness, who don't feel the pull for marriage, who don't see children as their understood future, all the snaps to you, my friends. We are better because you're here.

But as much as I wish I were that person who was totally content in singleness, I'm not. And as much as I wish I lived up to Paul's statement that it's better to be single, I cringe when that's thrown back at me because I hate that it's true.

I want to be married, and, unfortunately, I know I'm not alone. So maybe you're more like me, and you see this verse as permission to pursue the thing you desperately desire.

I encourage all of us in this camp to examine our motives. Are you pinning your hopes and dreams on a marriage? Have you downgraded your life to nothing more than a necessary segue to the altar? Are you racing toward the goal, and with each new dating app, relationship book, or matchmaking venture, sprinting down another detour, hoping it's the one that will lead you to the ribbon at the finish line?

We can't keep acting as if singleness is simply a phase or a season that we can hastily rush through if we make the right choice. This, as we all know, is not true.

What if singleness is all there is for you? What if you knew that, for whatever reason, God in his infinite glory and wisdom has seen fit for you to live a single life? How would that change your day to day? How much more could you start enjoying the journey instead of focusing on the destination?

Single, married, employed, job hunting, whoever you are, this life is a parade. And yes, you'll get flat tires on the float, and you'll forget the steps to that one part in the choreography, and you might even light that girl's hair on fire with your flaming baton, but that's what makes all this so much fun.

Take your eye off the finish line. I know, I know. It's harder than it sounds, especially for those of us who view marriage as a good and holy thing, but it is possible. When you do, when you're able to slow down and enjoy the show, you realize your success in this world is not defined by completing a race you never signed up for. You begin to understand that your singleness is not symptomatic of serious defects or irredeemable qualities. You can finally accept that no matter how you dance and twirl and sing along to the music, it won't move that float any faster, so you might as well enjoy the ride.

3

MARRIAGE CAN'T BE THE GREATEST SOURCE OF JOY

Once, I had a friend who cried.

This shouldn't be a noteworthy statement, except my friend never cried. When her first boyfriend broke up with her, she strapped on shin guards and went to soccer practice with a scowl firmly in place. As I sat beside her at her cousin's funeral, she was stoic. When she graduated with her master's (and later her doctorate), she beamed while walking across the stage, but that was the extent of her emotional gushing. Yet here she was, sitting across from me, telling stories from her honeymoon, and all the while, tears were streaming down her face.

"I didn't know I could be this happy," she said. And while she blew her nose, I cried a few tears of my own. Would I ever see this same happiness in my own life?

The church really likes for people to get married. And

that's wonderful—I want to be married too. But sometimes we might over-elevate the importance of marriage and undersell the work done in singleness. By that, I mean married people in the church seem to feel the need to do a kind of marriage PR all the time, keeping up a positive front so they don't damage the world's perception of marriage. As my friend Morgan says, "Topics become off-limits, and it's really hard to draw anything out of people about their marriages. But these are the most important people in our lives, and I want to know how that relationship is doing. But couples are very protective of all of that information."

Part of this PR is also seen in the under-the-surface messages married people perpetuate about the perks of having a marriage and family:

"My life started the day I met you."

"I've grown more spiritually in our two years together than I did in the twenty-three years before you."

"Being your bride has taught me more about Christ's love for his bride than I ever could have imagined."

I pulled these off social media in the last week. And depending on where you are in the singleness roller coaster, you may be grimacing, laughing, rolling your eyes, or crying right now. In the past I've had all these reactions to statements like this, because here's what they imply:

- Everything before your vows is a wash.
- All that work you're putting in spiritually can't really compete with the sanctification that comes in marriage.

- Being married gives you special insight into Jesus, salvation, and other spiritual matters.

What's sad is I know some married people who would actually nod along with those ideas. There is a deep, pervasive belief in the church that there's a unique kind of growth and maturity that can only come in marriage, that if you're single, your life hasn't really started yet, that marriage brings validity to your existence. Some churches refuse to hire single pastors because they question how a single man can minister to the needs of the married people, as if biblical insight and wisdom wane with prolonged singleness.

Man, we've gotten so much wrong. I'm sure I'll bring him up a lot, but it's with good reason: Paul, the man who wrote the majority of the New Testament, was single, and he offered all kinds of relational advice, some of which acts as the foundation for the vows we repeat in our ceremonies. What pastor would discredit his advice because Paul wasn't married? Or, as might be the case, would some pastors claim that Paul's advice, coming from a single man, is only authoritative because it's found in the inerrant Word of God?

I hope not. But this kind of undue celebrating of the effects of marriage has been indoctrinated in us since we were children. I have friends who can't use dishes in their hope chests because they're not married yet, despite the fact that as single women they'd still like to make nice homes. One woman I know is fitted every Christmas for her mother's wedding dress, and by the end of January the gown is taken in a half inch or the hem let out a little, just in case a wedding springs up in the next eleven months.

Not all of it is forced upon us though. Some of it we internalize by choice. By a certain age, many of us adopt this idea that marriage is the inevitable, estimable goal for our lives, and so the ways we choose to spend our time both reflect and reinforce this. I too strutted around in a veil when I was twelve and pretended to marry my poster of Jonathan Taylor Thomas (JB and JTT has a nice ring to it). In the past month alone I've watched no fewer than twenty-three Hallmark Christmas movies, and in each one the girl ends up with the guy, and my heart is ridiculously full and happy.

And I hate myself for it.

I wish I could shake off this idea that only in marriage will happiness come, that only in marriage will I grow into the best version of myself. It sure doesn't help when I give in to my desires and binge on cheesy romantic comedies, marinating in the underlying messages they proffer. And then I see those words on Facebook, and it all comes full circle. For a few years, I did battle with one particular lie that snuck in and wriggled into my brain; every week at church, I would be overwhelmed with the belief that my spiritual growth was stunted because I was single, because I couldn't experience the sanctification that comes with marriage. But if that's true, then Jesus and Paul and many of the priests and nuns who have supplied such rich theological work for us to study, alongside C. S. Lewis for much of his life and Nancy Leigh DeMoss Wolgemuth for much of hers, would all be out of the running for spiritual maturity. I suppose that's pretty decent company to keep.

JOY IS NOT SPELLED M-A-R-R-I-A-G-E

The myth of "marital bliss" has cast its shadow on the church, and we are all worse for it. If I unconsciously believe that marriage and family bring an elevated sense of joy and fulfillment, when I do get married, I will resent the heck out of a man who farts in his sleep and kids who drive me to drink. The reality of my situation will be unable to compare to this "bliss" I feel I am owed, and I will grow to believe I am an awful wife with an awful life and that I have been sold lies.

My friend Katelyn saw the products of this myth first-hand: "When working on my book, I found the constant refrain from women who stay home with children is 'This is not enough.' They love their children and husbands and homes, but they still feel this itch of something else. That was a signal to me that we've told women that being a wife and mom will be enough, but then they get to the other side of it, and they still feel this craving for something more."

What a disservice to ourselves and to the health of the church when we attach complete happiness and fulfillment to husbands and babies. In my quiet moments, the ones I very rarely voice, I sometimes wonder how many of my married friends feel so eager for me to tie the knot in part because they feel a certain level of jealousy over my life. Maybe it's under the surface, and they aren't even fully aware that they're seeking for me to make the same concessions they have. Then we can all pretend to be happy together, right?

I'm not the only one who feels pressure to be married. Katie, one of the sweetest, feistiest, and most beautiful women you'll ever meet, poured out her heart as a group of friends in Chicago discussed this very thing. "I feel like I have to defend my singleness and defend the fact that I am actually enjoying it," she said. "When someone tells me how I'd be great at being a wife or mom, it invalidates what I'm doing right now that feels valuable and life-giving, and those are things that don't depend on a man or children. People don't seem to trust me when I say I'm content. There's nothing wrong with that desire or hope, but you can't stake your life's fulfillment on a happy marriage."

And Katie would know, because she's been down this road before. "I had eight years between two engagements to learn that, well, hard stuff happens. It does. And it happens when you're not expecting it, and it comes in really painful ways. There aren't the guarantees that we're raised to think there are. And us asking these questions is not questioning God's character, but it's questioning what we've been handed down from family and the church. Life is too much of a wild card to hinge your hopes on marriage or biological children or whatever."

Our happiness cannot be conditionally tied to the dream of marriage and family. But too often, we end up having to do battle with loving friends and family members who insist we could be happier if only we found someone to spend our lives with. If only we got out more. If only we tried this new dating app. If only. These are exhausting relationships. And honestly, because of this implicit belief about marriage being the path to joy, I've found myself questioning the goodness of a God who could allow his children to sit in their singleness far longer than they'd desire. And that's when I realized that can't possibly be true.

INEXPRESSIBLE AND GLORIOUS

First Peter was written to the persecuted church, and in it I find a lot of comfort. In chapter 1, Peter digs into tribulations and the glory they produce:

> In all this you greatly rejoice, though now for a little while you may have had to suffer grief in all kinds of trials. These have come so that the proven genuineness of your faith—of greater worth than gold, which perishes even though refined by fire—may result in praise, glory and honor when Jesus Christ is revealed. Though you have not seen him, you love him; and even though you do not see him now, you believe in him and are filled with an inexpressible and glorious joy, for you are receiving the end result of your faith, the salvation of your souls. (v. 6–9 NIV)

Though my plight of singleness can hardly compare to the trials of the persecuted church, Peter could have written this passage to me. In my head, I read the first bit like this: "In your life, you find reason to rejoice, even though your singleness has caused suffering. These trials have come so that when your faith is tested it may result in praise, glory, and honor when Jesus Christ is revealed."

But the second half of that section doesn't need reworking, which is exactly my point: "Though you have not seen him, you love him; and even though you do not see him now, you believe in him and are filled with an inexpressible and glorious joy." Inexpressible and glorious joy. That's exactly what my friend was describing as she sniffled over snap-shots taken in the Caribbean, but here, that indescribable joy comes from knowing and loving Jesus.

In my singleness I have come to know and love God. I have come to see him in the warmth of friends, in the distance my dollar stretches, and in the timely hug of an acquaintance. I have grown closer to him in the suffering that singleness brings, the nights spent alone and wondering if this is all there is. I know him through his Word, through my pastors, his messengers, and through his people. My singleness has driven me into the arms of my Father as I flounder around in this world, physically alone but spiri-tually supported.

It is a great comfort, then, to know that my singleness, the thorn in my flesh that has fueled my dependence on God, has produced a knowledge of him, which gave birth to a love, and that love makes room for joy. Inexpressible and glorious joy. Praise God!

Everything I need for that joy, everything I need to attain spiritual maturity, everything I need to grow in wis-dom and in strength and in love is right here. I don't have to be married to be wise. I don't have to be a mother to have supernatural love. I don't have to own a home to be hospitable.

"You can do anything for the kingdom! You live for the kingdom, and you can die for the kingdom," says Jazzy, a twenty-five-year-old volunteer who works with college stu-dents. "You're not tied to anything but the kingdom. You can live your life fiercely, rather than sitting around and waiting."

Fiercely living. Can you even imagine what that would look like? Sometimes I take in my delivered pizzas and Netflix binges, and I wonder if this is what Jazzy was talking about. Probably not, but the crazy part is I could change that at any moment. This life is mine to live (or to waste), and its potential is not determined by a spouse or children.

WASTE OF RESOURCES

Here's the hard part of this conversation, the part that I'd gloss over if I could, but I can't because this book is about addressing all the things we've been avoiding.

I'll let Jeanean start us off: "A lot of people define us by our singleness because, for many of us, our singleness doesn't look like sacrifice—it looks like selfishness. And it doesn't look like sanctification—it looks like me doing all my own stuff. We need to own up to what our singleness was supposed to be used for. I'm not going to see the value of singleness if the biggest thing I see is singles not serving."

Oof. I'll say right now that I don't know your circumstances, I don't know how you're using your time, and I don't know if this applies to you. But I do know that for me, life holds a lot of wasted hours. For years, I wandered around the Chicagoland areas on Sunday mornings because I couldn't find a church I liked enough to get plugged into. I always meant to find a ministry and volunteer, but that was put on the back burner. I, of course, wanted to find outlets for my let-me-love-you complex, but dinners with friends and a general preoccupation with my life left me with little to spare.

In that respect, I'm sure some of my married friends were growing more spiritually and experiencing more joy than I was, but not because they were married and I was single. It's because they were investing in intimate relationships that forced them to give of themselves, that forced them to think of other people and adjust their schedules and desires (as marriage and motherhood often demand of someone). Being single can make you selfish. It can stunt your spiritual growth—but it doesn't have to. This is why seeking out community, being held accountable, and forcing yourself to go to that thing and volunteer for that event are vital to your spiritual health.

On the flip side, as important as it is for us to use our singleness in a way that fosters growth and community and selflessness, it's equally important for the church to recognize that all of these things are possible for us as well.

Sitting around a table in Nashville, Jaycelyn opened up about a common response she receives: "One of the hardest parts about being single is when I feel like other people believe my life hasn't started yet. I had a patient's father the other day offer to pray for me—to get married. It was the first thing on his mind, *Oh, she's not married. That's a problem.*"

Heather has experienced a similar sense of judgment and isolation, even from well-meaning people in her life. "Many of my friends are married, so even at game night, I make it an odd number," she says. "And I always feel like their husbands are a little strange around me; they're hesitant to get too close—even though I love sports and it's easier for me to talk to men. I often feel like if my husband were standing there with me, I wouldn't be as threatening. Being in a relationship would make me safer."

When singleness is viewed as something to be treated, to be prayed away, or to be scared of, it only exacerbates the insecurity singles already feel. We need the church to stop acting as though singles are defective ("If only you could become more confident in speaking to guys") or degenerate ("You'll understand this kind of thing more once you're married"). And good grief, guys, sharing the love seat with your wife's best friend is not going to result in an affair.

Even the programming in our churches needs to be reconsidered. As Heather says, "A lot of ministries in the church are geared toward married women and mothers. The Bible studies that are on Tuesday at 9:00 a.m. Even a lot of the events tend to be baby showers and bridal showers. Not every woman gets married or has a baby, but her life is still worth validating."

If you're teaching third grade and waiting tables in the summer, your life is still worth validating. If you're healing from a broken engagement, suffocating under the disappointment of everyone around you, your life is still worth validating. If you've never had a boyfriend or even been on a date and you don't even have a thriving career to show for it, your life is still worth validating.

We've limited ourselves in what we choose to honor in the church. I'd love to see churches acknowledge when someone finally earns that black belt, decides to buy that house, takes that big promotion, or signs that book deal.

When I was in grad school, I lived with my best friends. We watched trashy reality TV, shared Japanese takeout food, and became deeply invested in the accomplishments of the entire group. Birthdays were observed with abandon. Surviving our first semester teaching was cause for a night on the town. And when I successfully defended my master's thesis, there were balloons and cards and dinner options and a group of smiling faces waiting for me when I got home. My life has significance, and the presence of my friends and their celebration of my life underscored that truth for me.

WHAT IT ALL MEANS FOR YOU

It's easy to believe you're far behind the curve. When siblings start having babies and friends get married and your closet is full of bridesmaid dresses (that you'll *totally* wear again), it's hard to remember your life is important and filled with significant milestones as well.

I have friends who are on second babies and even second marriages, but here I am, attending yet another shower for them while my life still feels as if it's in the same place. But it's not. In that same amount of time I've gotten promotions (and gotten fired) and deepened relationships and traveled the country. I've attended conferences on foster care and I've gone through intense therapy. I've volunteered in youth groups and watched my baby niece for hours. I have lived a lot of life, and it's a discredit to me and to what God is doing in and through me to refuse to acknowledge that. And it's the same for you.

Your life is valid and valuable, and your spiritual maturity is not limited by your singleness. True faith always keeps good company. Joy and peace and kindness and goodness are not far behind when faith is leading. Let's cling to this truth. Let no man despise your youth or your marital status, because the work you can do, the lives that you can change, the hope you can have is not dictated by a marriage that you cannot attain (and may not even want).

Again: being single isn't indicative of stunted emotional or spiritual growth, and it's not a reflection of something being broken inside you, though I know it often feels that way. About once a year I sit down with my closest friends (and any man who will answer), and I ask the same questions: "Why am I still single? Is there some huge thing that no one is telling me but you all understand is really the reason I'm not married?"

Even if there were a *thing* (apart from my predilection for eating chips in my sandwich), it wouldn't matter because people with *things* get married all the time. Folks with horrible hygiene and rude communication styles and a general lack of wit have managed to find mates, and this fact is both humbling and helpful for me.

At the end of the day, someone else's failure to choose and love you properly does not make you a failure. You have to learn to love yourself, to believe you are capable of joy and spiritual growth and wisdom in your singleness, and that you are worthy of these things and that you are worthy of love.

Many of us feel marginalized by the church's push for marriage, but I would encourage you now more than ever to lean into your churches. Find community there, even when it requires much of you. Push through the awkward initial dinners and interactions, seek out families (even though it'd be awfully nice if they met you halfway), build intimacy with people who will challenge and sharpen you. Give someone the spare key to your house. Invite yourself over. Impose. And when all else fails, bring pie. Nobody can turn down a good piece of pie.

4

JESUS MIGHT NOT MEET ALL YOUR NEEDS

"When once we get intimate with Jesus we are never lonely, we never need sympathy, we can pour out all the time without being pathetic."[1] Oswald Chambers wrote this in *My Utmost for His Highest*, a work that has shaped my spiritual life in more ways than I can count. But on this point, Mr. Chambers, I humbly disagree.

If nothing else, my singleness has taught me that you can be lonely and exhausted and in need of sympathy—even with God. Even Jesus felt this way, and in the days and moments leading to his crucifixion, we see this played out. I can think of no greater loneliness than hanging on a cross, dying for a world that despises you, and then feeling forsaken by the Father who sent you, but—glory be!—loneliness and exhaustion did not cause Jesus to crumble.

We have deep needs, you and I. Some needs are so deep and cavernous only God himself can crawl into those places, those dark corners, and abide there, bringing light with him. We're created with needs, needs that people and friends and lovers are meant to fill. Not to say the Lord couldn't meet these needs, but their purpose is to drive us toward something greater than our individual selves and separate from God. While many, like Oswald Chambers, would argue that Jesus will meet all of your needs, even if you never get married, I'm not sure that's true. I know he can, but the question is if he will.

A HOLY MATRIMONY

I still remember the day I was first betrothed. I was visiting a friend's youth group, and all of us took our True Love Waits rings, signed our cards, and one woman made a statement that I can still hear ringing in my ears: "Now you're married to Jesus."

Wait . . . what?

That's not *exactly* what I had signed up for. I was all for sexual purity, especially since no boy had even tried to hold my hand, and the silver ring was pretty cute. But I never agreed to marry Jesus. I still don't even know what that means.

But that sweet woman with her smile and homemade banana bread voiced an idea into my soul that I could never really shake: *If I am without a husband, Jesus steps in to fill this void. Jesus can meet this need.* After all, if he is a father to the fatherless, he is a husband to the husbandless.

This idea is only perpetuated through the Christianese we use, especially in praise and worship songs. Let me tell you, I'm right there with you, swaying in the dark with the lights turned down, my heart beating along with the resonating kick drum, tears streaming down my face as I sing about the Lord's hurricane of jealousy and sloppy wet kisses. The songs we sing in church are filled with this imagery.

> *"I want to touch You . . . I want to know*
> *You more."*[2]
> *"You are more beautiful than anyone ever."*[3]
> *"I need You, oh, I need You."*[4]
> *"I'm falling even more in love with You,*
> *letting go of all I've held onto."*[5]
> *"Near Him I always will be, for nothing can*
> *keep me away. He is my destiny."*[6]

Oh, whoops, that last one is a lyric from "I Will Follow Him," definitely not a song about Jesus (despite Whoopi singing a smashing rendition of it as a nun in *Sister Act*). But clearly the mistake is easy enough to make.

I'd be thrilled if these words were written or said about me, and I've cried them out to God more times than I care to admit. For heaven's sake, I have a tattoo that actually reads "beloved" in Hebrew, and for years I referred to it as my brand from the Lord, that I was his and he is mine. Trust me, I get why we buy into this—I do. I want to be a

Disney princess pursued by a prince. I want to be fought for and chased after. I want to be romanced. But I don't think that's Jesus' job.

ROMANCING THE SAVIOR?

Unfortunately, I feel like I'm in the minority here. As a college freshman, I remember meeting up with a girl from my hall for coffee. When I got to Starbucks, I saw her red-rimmed eyes and knew that things must have ended with Dave, her boyfriend of three months and two days.

I bought us pumpkin spice lattes (because calories don't count in the forty-eight hours post breakup), and I sat down, ready to tear into this guy who had broken my friend's heart. But before I could finish my tirade about the immaturity of freshman boys, my friend stopped me. "No, no, it was me," she said, her eyes welling up again. "I know that I need to take some time and be with Jesus for a while."

Unbelievable. I'm chatting up every unattached male in the incoming class of 2007, trying to score a husband at the world's largest Christian university, and she cut a catch loose so she could date *Jesus*? Don't get me wrong—I like Jesus too, but let's not be hasty.

My friend is not alone in viewing Jesus this way. I once heard a Sunday school teacher describe how handsome Jesus must have been with his beard and robes. Those thonged sandals really get some women going, I guess.

So we date Jesus, he romances us, and then we marry him, the handsome groom who relentlessly pursues his beloved.

WOULD CARS BREAK DOWN IN
THE GARDEN OF EDEN?

But this theology fell apart for me. After coming home on yet another college break without a boyfriend, I'd have people in my life, whom I respect, tell me things like, "All you need to do is press into Jesus. Focus on your relationship with him. He'll meet all your needs." So I tried to force Jesus into this role of boyfriend and sole provider of relational needs, but it left me empty, and my heart became fallow.

Jesus does not meet all my relational needs. And some of you are already shutting this book and calling me a heretic, but I would, with all loving-kindness, point you to the very beginning of the world.

You remember the passage we discussed earlier? You know, with Adam, the first man that God created. God, in all his power and glory, looked at Adam, whom he planned to commune with for all of eternity in the garden of Eden, guiding, leading, and sustaining him, and he said that it was not good for man to be alone.

But Adam wasn't alone! He had God—the meeter of all needs! The ultimate companion! But God had created Adam with a need for something more than what God himself was supposed to meet—a need for community, for others, for relationships. We're all created this way; introvert and extrovert alike, we need people.

For a few years I forgot all about Genesis 1. I forgot that we're created with relational wants that others are supposed to meet for us, and I forgot about that whole iron-sharpens-iron thing.[7] I forgot about the ultimate example of flourishing community found in Acts, and I forgot that even Jesus had his disciples. Instead, I focused solely on the Lord—on finding complete fulfillment in him. I sequestered myself, I turned inward, I prayed and fasted and waited on the Lord to romance my soul. And I'm still waiting. (But no longer fasting—girl's gotta eat.) God used this time to teach me many things, and one of them was how foolish I had been.

I am but one part of a whole. I am the right hand's pinkie finger that completely ignored the fact that I am sustained and made stronger by the other parts of this body. And, at the end of the day, I'm sanctified through those relationships—through selflessly loving others until I'm tired and broken, and then the Lord fills me back up *to do it all over again.*

When Jesus compared himself and his bride to a husband and wife, it was always in the context of selfless submission, not romance and wooing. He wasn't telling husbands how to light candles and whisper sweet nothings; he was teaching them how to lead and give of themselves. And while the Lord speaks differently to each of us, he's never wooed me—not once.

Honestly, while Jesus is my only hope, sometimes I need a handyman. Jesus has never fixed my broken washing machine or come to put the door back on my closet. He's never changed my oil, helped me dig out my car in six feet of snow, or jumped my car battery in the middle of a rainstorm while my windows were down. But many of my brothers and sisters in Christ have stepped in and met these needs.

Jesus has never made me dinner or given me a hug after

a long day. He's never held my hand in the car or surprised me with a little surcee just because. But people have. They've loved me well. And only when I gave up the expectation of Jesus filling a role that he never promised to fill did I stop feeling ashamed and embarrassed for still being dissatisfied.

That's why we need to stop perpetuating this idea that Jesus can meet relational needs when there is a deficit. It sounds so beautiful, and it plays perfectly into our romance-driven culture that craves a happy ending, but this is simply not true. When there is a relational deficit, Jesus will fill it—with another person, or, if you're lucky enough, with many of them.

SINGLE TOGETHER, THAT'S A THING NOW

"You know what's hard for me? The Christianese and gimmicks behind singleness in the church." Patty, who also heads up a young singles ministry at her church, started chatting while there was a lull in conversation. "Because of the language we use, I find it difficult to view my singleness in a healthy way. Singleness isn't only your status quo; it's your *significance*. My friends like to say 'single together,' because we don't like the word *single*. Really, I don't like anything single, not even my cheeseburgers."

Amen, Patty. Amen. Only through banding together in this way, coming together at tables and on couches and in pews, can we actually fill those relational needs we were created with. *Single together* is far better than *single alone*.

Using Patty's comment as a springboard, Deb, a licensed

counselor, hit at the heart of the issue: "Where the church is failing is they're not addressing community and what it really means to be in community. If we look at the biblical examples of marriage, they're pretty limited. It's been interesting for me, as I'm striving to find my independence, to be forced into intimate community, even when it was against my will. I went through a time where I was relying on close friends to financially support me and provide me a place to live. Now my roommate and I live in an apartment without walls, which is totally God-driven. Our apartment is an artist's loft in this very rich, artistic community, so we've learned how to have lots of conversations and to communicate and to fight because neither one of us can go to our room and slam the door. When the church talks about marriage, they do overemphasize it. But I don't think the failure is not addressing singleness more; the failure is not addressing community more."

Community is so incredibly hard to build. It takes time and effort and sacrifice. It requires laying down your own desires and your idea of a perfectly clean kitchen and your dinner plans to accommodate other fundamentally flawed people, but that's what we're called to do. An empty table holds opportunity. Potential relationships. Conversations yet to be had. As we see modeled throughout the New Testament, tables serve their intended purpose when people come together, with Christ in their midst, to cultivate relationships, bear one another's burdens, and live charitably with one another.

Community doesn't mean joining with ten other prototypes of yourself. Jeanean, a mentor and writer out of the

Chicago area, pushed the discussion further: "Community has to be intermingled. Many times my brothers in the faith don't know what's going on. And we, as women, don't know how our brothers think or feel. We need relationships with them in order to understand." So many times in the past few years I've had to trust the people around me and discount my own perception or opinion, whether it's in dealing with issues of race or politics or even in how men perceive me. If I'm not getting that outside perspective, how am I supposed to learn where my blind spots are?

Community is only as rich and deep as it is diverse. When we limit ourselves to a whole bunch of people who are exactly like us, we're limiting the refining power of community not only to meet needs but also to sanctify. Find friends who look different from you, who work in different areas, who value different things, who are older than you. These voices can speak truth into your life, truth you may have missed.

RELATIONSHIP STATUS: WE'RE BETTER THAN THIS

So often I have the best intentions for cultivating a dynamic community, but these efforts can be thwarted by something as innocuous as small talk. If left to my own devices and natural inclinations, I would be surrounded by a swarm of girls who drink wine, giggle their way through *Gilmore Girls*, and only talk about boys. That's where I'm comfortable. That doesn't challenge or hurt me. But almost always, these conversations fail what's known as the Bechdel test. This test is a good measure for films: two women, who must be named, have to have a conversation about something other than a man. About 50 percent of our movies pass these very basic standards, which I feel is more than could be said for my own conversations.

"I get so mad at some of my female friendships," said Morgan Lee, an editor at *Christianity Today*. "The problem is that many of my own conversations and 'scenes' fail the Bechdel test that I hold my movies to. And that is infuriating to me, because I have very close friends who are doing very interesting things with their lives. I want to talk about those things. If you're going to your job every day, why are we not talking about that and supporting each other there?"

If we're not asking those important questions—the ones that dig deeper than "Is he cute?" and "How'd the date go?"—who is? I like comparing notes on OkCupid matches as much as the next girl, especially when it turns out that the guy I was talking to in Muncie, Indiana, some 337 miles away, was also talking to my coworker—a fun fact unearthed at happy hour one night. But we've got to be more than our dating profiles and Friday-night plans. We are more interesting than the latest guy we've been talking to, and it's time we believe that and start acting like it.

I'M EMOTIONALLY AND SPIRITUALLY STUNTED . . . I THINK

Singleness is hard for a lot of different reasons, but fear plays an undeniable role. We all are struggling with, working around, and ignoring different fears that creep in when we're home alone watching *Love Actually* for the tenth time, wishing for our own man with cue cards and recorded carolers.

Katelyn brought up one common fear toward the end of our discussion in Chicago, pointing to, as she put it, "that 'I'm going to die alone' fear. Which is a legitimate one. *I wonder if I'm going to get to the end of my life without a companion, without someone knowing me intimately.* And because of that real fear, people get married—maybe to the wrong people—and they realize they're not a strong match. But it's better than being alone. If the church were to live in that community that we see in Acts, we would actually have better, stronger marriages, because we're getting married for the right reasons, not only to solve the loneliness problem." Our fears not only affect us, they influence the choices we make, the culture we're creating, the churches we have, and the lies we're feeding. Fears are powerful, and for most single women, fears are unavoidable.

While Katelyn fears dying alone (valid), I fear dying as less-than—dying as less developed, less accomplished, less mature, less able, less happy, a *less* version of myself because I was never married. Because I so fervently believe that one of the purposes of marriage is sanctification, one of my deepest fears is that I can only reach a limited level of holiness apart from marriage. And I feel as if there's an emotional well or depth that can only be tapped by motherhood and marriage, one that I won't be able to access apart from these avenues. And these two things scare me to death.

But God is teaching me that this fear is totally justified . . . if I'm not living in community. I am limited in my sanctification if there is no other iron to sharpen me. I will be emotionally dead and restricted if I don't recklessly pour myself out for other people. See, marriage isn't the *only* thing that sanctifies—it simply *also* sanctifies. Community can play the same role in my life. My fears are only founded when I limit myself to retreating to Jesus and rejecting the people he has placed around me.

I don't know what your fears are today; I don't know what you're struggling with. Maybe it's that you're one of those, like me, who has to rely on the help of people who don't rely on you. When I'm constantly having to ask people to do things for me, to fix things, or even to lend me money, that's embarrassing. But I'm not completely independent, and I can't pretend I am. And maybe feeling embarrassed is a good way to keep me humble.

Or maybe you long to share your life with someone. You want a person, your person, with whom you can download the day every evening, sharing those little pieces of minutia that only someone who loves you would care about. You want someone to do everyday life with, to go shopping with, to take road trips with. None of these desires are bad, but I don't think we can keep expecting Jesus to meet them. In fact, he's given us the means to meet them. We can find them all in community (at least in some capacity).

I challenge you to ask yourself, *What am I hinging myself on?* We don't like to think of ourselves as relying on anything, so the language of dependency can be off-putting. But just as a door is hinged to the wall—we're all hinging ourselves to something. We're anchoring ourselves, our identity, our worth, our strength, to something (or a few things). Whether it's work or activism or family or relationships, we're drilling those holes and tightening the screws.

So, what are you hinging yourself to? Is it an unfulfilling relationship with Christ because you've painted him as your boyfriend when he wants to be your Savior? Is it shallow relationships with girlfriends that revolve around your latest dates and your shared passion for documentaries? Or maybe you're like me, and you're starting to hinge yourself on community, on being broken with other people, on learning to love others even when it hurts.

If you want to be defined by more than your singleness, then you need to convey that through your conversations and priorities. When you reduce yourself to the want—or pursuit—of a husband, you are choosing to define yourself by what you lack instead of what you are.

I'm learning that in my singleness, I actually have so much more—more time, more resources, more opportunity to pour myself into the relationships around me. I can take calls in the middle of the night from friends. I can hop in the car for a weekend trip to help with two new foster baby placements. I can contribute to a GoFundMe for seminary books. I have a deep capacity for friendship, perhaps even deeper than that of my married friends, and that is a gift that comes with this time in my life, a gift I benefit from every single day. Singleness and intimacy are not at odds, despite the messaging we've received.

Tim Keller, whom I adore and argue could be a writer in the biblical canon, lays down some serious truth in *The Meaning of Marriage*: "To be loved but not known is comforting but superficial. To be known and not loved is our greatest fear. But to be fully known and truly loved is, well, a lot like being loved by God. It is what we need more than anything. It liberates us from pretense, humbles us out of our self-righteousness, and fortifies us for any difficulty life can throw at us."[8]

To be loved and to be known. That is what you were made for. That is what Christ promises you—through himself *and* community. This life is hard—too hard to weather alone. Whether you view Jesus as that strapping young pirate with Fabio hair on the front of a romance novel or whether you view him as a kind, old, gentlemanly grandfather with a pipe and snuffbox, know that man destined you for himself and for other people, and to forget either one of those is to miss your entire purpose.

5

SORRY, GOD MIGHT NOT GIVE YOU YOUR HEART'S DESIRES

A hunky, six-foot-three, flannel-wearing, beard-growing, Jesus-loving CEO, that's what Jesus wants for me. Do you know how I know? Because I was taught long ago if I was seeking the Lord, genuinely seeking to know and love and glorify him, he would morph my heart—he would strip it of everything that wasn't pleasing to him, and he would infuse it with his desires for my life.

Praise him! I love the Lord, and I have given him reign in my heart, and I still want to marry a hunky, six-foot-three, flannel-wearing, beard-growing, Jesus-loving CEO. Therefore, that desire must be from Jesus, right? After all, that's what I was promised.

Psalm 37:4 says, "Delight yourself in the LORD, and he will give you the desires of your heart." I remember sitting in the pew of my church as a young girl while the pastor preached a whole sermon on this single verse. Over and over, he drew the distinction between the desires of the flesh and the desires of the Spirit. This passage, he argued, isn't validating a prosperity gospel. Instead, it's saying if you hand over your heart and life to Jesus, he'll change your desires—he'll morph them into his desires. Suddenly you won't want to drink anymore, your flesh won't crave that illicit substance, and you won't desire to listen to that music with the satanic backbeat. (Fundamentalism in the nineties, y'all.)

This interpretation made a lot of sense to me. When I fell in love with a boy when I was nineteen and he was uninterested, I prayed like never before for God to change my heart, for him to strip away these emotions and remove the attraction. Months later, I was still praying that same prayer, but the time in between had riddled me with self-doubt and insecurity.

I couldn't genuinely love the Lord if he couldn't change my heart's desires. I couldn't be as sold out for Christ as I thought I was if all of my waking moments were spent strategically placing myself in well-trafficked areas in our school in order to catch a glimpse of my beloved. Could I?

I assumed if the Lord changes my desires as I learn to love him, there was clearly a spiritual defect in me that he was working out. I became obsessed with those personality tests that tell you more about yourself (ESFJ, 2-wing-3, Woo and Maximizer, and Leslie Knope with a pinch of Donna). I knew if I did the hard work of scouring my heart and soul, the Lord would reveal the hidden sin in my life—and consequently deliver the very attractive boy in my biology class straight to me.

I found through this process that too much self-reflection led to self-obsession. After years of wondering what kind of character deficiency or unknown flaw would cause the Lord to keep a husband from me, I realized it doesn't really work that way. That's turning the God of the universe into a Coca-Cola machine that exists to dispense happiness.

Delighting in God, as that verse in Psalms says, is a responsibility and gift. And at the end of the day, I appreciate what Matthew Henry's commentary says about this passage. He doesn't endorse the prosperity gospel interpretation, and he doesn't back my pastor's view of a heart that is shaped around God's desires. Rather, Matthew Henry wrote, "What is the desire of the heart of a good man? It is this, to know, and love, and live to God, to please him and to be pleased in him."[1]

The only desire with guaranteed delivery in this life is God himself: "Draw near to God, and he will draw near to you" (James 4:8). That's it—and that's everything we'll ever need.

YOU CAN'T HURRY (OR EARN) LOVE

I can't help my deep and abiding desire for marriage—it's something that's in me, and even though its potency ebbs and flows, the desire always remains. I've recently decided I'm not going to be embarrassed by that desire. I'm not going to view it as a spiritual flaw, and I'm also not going to see it as a weakness. Some people want to start their own businesses, some want to work with their hands all day, some want to knit and watch *Wheel of Fortune*, and I desperately want to be married and to be a mom to a van full of children I'm convinced are demon-possessed as they scream and cry and smear paint on the walls. Coming to this point of acceptance took a lot of work. I've found owning desire makes others uncomfortable. I've told people, "I want to be married," and on more than one occasion I've been met with "That makes you sound a little desperate." Ouch.

This is why people aren't forthcoming. If we can't even give voice to our God-honoring desires, how on earth can we pursue them in a healthy, honest way? We have to make space for this kind of dialogue in the church. We have to allow room for longing, for confession, for intimacy.

Part of this culture of criticism surrounding singleness comes in the implicit judgment that if a person is single later in life (and by that, I mean after the age of twenty-five), there must be something wrong with him or her—single for a reason, as opposed to single for a season. We think this about the unmarried people we meet—it's an immediate judgment that goes off in my head as I try and evaluate the broken piece, performing a sort of diagnostic test: "Are you employed? Oh, huh . . . Are you active in church? Okay, that's good . . . Do you wear dad jeans on a regular basis?"

But the truth is that many of us do have defects and flaws. We have unflattering clothes and annoying habits, but so do those sweet couples who somehow ended up married. Part of reworking the narrative comes in refusing to believe that a person is at fault for her own singleness. This is one of the underlying assumptions in the flawed thinking we currently accept without question. Even as single people, we've digested this and believe it to be true.

"Why am I not married yet—why can't I find a husband?"

I've heard this countless times from my friends. And in the past year, as I've experienced two almost-relationships that have fallen apart in the final days before what would have surely been a very successful DTR, I've asked this question a hundred times myself.

As Catalina, a twenty-seven-year-old visual artist, mentioned at our roundtable in Chicago, "When we operate under the assumption that all roads lead to marriage, we start viewing ourselves through the eyes of men, not God. And that's when our emotions get trapped, when they come in waves: *Does this guy like me? Am I marryable? How am I being perceived?*"

And I understand the impetus here. When you're aiming for marriage, you make sure that every possible roadblock is removed. *If it's the way I'm dressing, I'll buy new clothes. If it's a lack of maturity, I'll grow up. If it's an absence of spark, I'll Google some interesting facts and practice witty banter that I'll covertly weave into conversation during our date.*

As Catalina says, "We're not called to fear men or even ourselves. We're called to have our identity in Christ, to see ourselves how Christ sees us—and to see other people how Christ sees them." It sounds simple, but we're still getting lost along the way.

How do we love ourselves when we feel so unlovable? And what is making us so hard to love? These questions run deep in our souls. They multiply and reverberate, picking up speed, until the only choice is to say the words aloud or allow them to tear us apart.

It's easy to understand why we, like sweet Anne of

Green Gables before us, buy cheap goods from a peddler on the street to change the way we look. But instead of dye to make our red hair raven black, we've bought the lie that God's putting a husband on pause until we've reached a certain point. But much like Anne's, our purchase is a sham. Instead of green hair, though, we end up with empty promises and insecurity.

"God's waiting for you to be ready. He's doing a work in you, and then he's going to bring that man along."

Friends, that is a lie—it's not biblical, and we have to do everything in our power to root this idea out of the church and out of our advice and out of our thoughts. God is not waiting until you are ready to bring a spouse.

If I believed God were doing this, it would undermine everything I know to be true about grace and mercy and righteousnesses that are like filthy rags because I can do nothing to earn salvation, I can do nothing to earn the love of God, and I can do nothing to earn a husband. While it might not sound like that's what your friends' bad advice is claiming, it's exactly what it's offering: *Become more holy, more ready, and God will reward you with a husband. He's holding out until you get your life straightened out. God's keeping a good thing from you in order to improve your behavior or your spiritual walk, but once that's in check, he's going to lavish you with a healthy marriage and a happy family.*

Nope. That's not right. That is, at its core, another version of the prosperity gospel we're all so quick to discount. Thomas Umstattd Jr. calls it the *relational* prosperity gospel, and he nailed it:

The tragedy of both the financial and relational prosperity gospels is that when someone is going through hard times, it is "a sign" that they don't have enough faith. The more we believe in the prosperity gospel, the more we tend to sound like the Pharisees who said the reason the man was born blind was because of his parents' sin. . . .

The reality is that our actions have consequences. Bad actions can have bad consequences and good actions can have good consequences. The key word here is "can." If we are not in full control of the world how can all the consequences in our lives be our fault? Laziness does make you hungry (Proverbs 19:15). But do you know what else will make you hungry? A famine. And sometimes famines are not your fault.[2]

We do not have to reach a certain level of maturity or spiritual or personal growth so God can see we're worthy of (and ready for) marriage. Marriage is meant to sanctify us—why would we have to attain spiritual perfection in order for that to be delivered? None of us is ready for marriage, and none of us has spiritually arrived.

GOD'S NOT A GENIE

Viewing God as a dispensary for wishes is, quite honestly, heretical, and I believe it undermines the gospel. Our spiritual lives aren't transactional. The Lord isn't punishing bad behavior or rewarding good. He is bringing glory to himself in all things.

God does not operate on this gold-star reward system. "I will give it all to you if you will worship me" (Luke 4:7 NLT) is not printed in red letters in your Bible for a reason. Jesus never made this claim—but Satan did. Just as the Devil tried to woo Jesus with his own version of a prosperity gospel, we have been wooing singles in the church with this idea that if only we were better (better looking, better acting, better loving), God would see fit to deliver a spouse.

I wouldn't bank on this. I'm not going to behave or perform in a certain way and hold God to "his end of the bargain." I'm not going to grow spiritually only with the hopes that one day I become worthy of a husband. I'm not going to give into the lie that I don't have a man because I don't deserve one.

In reality, singleness is a gift to the church, one that we should stop trying to return. Singleness is not meant to be pitied, shamed, fixed, or even ignored. It is to be celebrated. And when we imply that we are still single because we are lacking in some way, we spit in the face of Paul, who wrote that it's better to be single than to be married—and he lived a life that spoke to this truth.

THE REALITY OF UNFULFILLED DESIRES

"The hardest part of being single is being a single Christian," Katelyn told a group of us. "Mainstream culture has more positive models of living a full life as a person who's not married. In the evangelical Christian community, we perpetuate messages like 'marriage is God's best for you' or 'marriage is a reward for your faithfulness,' or we center our churches on married families. All these things start to raise really hard questions about God's goodness and providence. In some ways, there's an additional level of pain or spiritual woundedness that can arise when you start asking, 'Where is God in all of this?' and you're met with silence from a church culture that doesn't always know how to answer that question in a helpful, constructive, or freeing way."

If God's not withholding a man to make me ready, what is he waiting on? And what does it say about God that he's keeping a good thing from me, despite my fervent desires? How do I honor and serve a God who has the power to change my circumstances but chooses not to, causing me immense loneliness and pain?

These are my questions, and I don't have any answers—except to say God is good and God is in control. Some days those are enough for me to help me nod my head, take a deep breath, and keep plugging along. And some days they're not. Some days those answers leave me throwing my pillow against a wall or weeping into the phone while my brother anxiously tries to decipher my wails and pauses as if they were Morse code.

But at the end of the day, those are the two pillars that hold up my entire faith: God is good. God is in control. In 2016 I was let go from a job, twice, and in both instances people came to support me with the same predictable phrases: "There's something better headed your way!" and "When God closes one door, he opens a window." But the tough reality is that there are people who love the Lord and honor him with their lives, and they've been out of work for more than a year, or they had to take a demotion and pay cut to get another job. There are single women who will serve God with everything, desperately desire companionship, and never be "rewarded" with an earthly marriage—and God is still good.

I take comfort that Jesus never encouraged us to deny the cross we're called to carry. He never tells us to ignore the cross, to imagine the cross as being featherlight, or to try to pass it off to someone else. No, he simply says, "Take up your cross, and follow me." You don't have to deny the existence of your cross, whatever it may be—you only have to take it up. I don't have to deny that I desire marriage or that in my singleness there is suffering. But I am called to endure this time with grace, humility, patience, and joy. Some days I'm convinced singleness is too great a thing to ask of someone who wants to be married, but I take up my cross and continue on, day by day, step by step. And as I stumble under the weight of the wood and scrape my knees, and it feels too heavy to bear, there in those moments, crumpled under the cross, Jesus finds me. And he'll find you too.

If you're single, you're called to be single today, and I will grieve and celebrate that calling with you. We must embrace it. But that doesn't mean our hearts won't want more. Own that pain and heartache. Don't deny it. Don't push it aside. Sit in it. And then, when you're able, look up. Find God in the longing.

I have said it before, but I will keep saying it, because we need to hear it: marriage is not indicative of maturation—and singleness is not symptomatic of infantilism. Being single does not mean you are less-than, wanting, or insufficient.

If you are single, do not assume it's because you need to prepare more for marriage or you're inherently unlovable. These are all lies.

Label them as such, and embrace the truth: Your capacity for joy, spiritual growth, influence, and belonging are not limited by your relationship status. You are deeply valued, intentionally created, wholly loved, and fully known—these things are not dependent on vows taken at an altar.

May we strive to live in these truths and, when necessary, expel the lies that cause our holy longing for marriage to be marred by deep feelings of inadequacy.

"GUARD YOUR HEART"

One of the lies we have to kill is the idea that we can change our desires by guarding our hearts. This phrase has become a propaganda tool that only encourages us to insulate ourselves from pain.

Over and over, youth pastors and parents and friends have told me to guard my heart (with good reason, since I am quite likely to hand it away to strangers, vagabonds, and not-nice men). But I do wonder if this too has contributed to the problem. I'm only now learning the difference between using discernment and remaining distant.

In a bid to guard my heart, I've constructed a rather ridiculous mirage of a man I'll never find, complete with deal-breakers and marriage-makers, and I've called this wisdom. Unfortunately, I'm not alone. I don't know a single girl who doesn't have at least a few basic necessities jotted down on a mental spreadsheet, ready to help her analyze and itemize the next guy who comes along. But too often these lists of ideals become unrealistic, more closely resembling a spiritual superhero than a God-fearing man.

As much as I can pray for a guy with financial stability, spiritual thirst, confidence, and a desire to adopt, I can only hope there's a man praying for a girl from a broken home with a bum knee and mild social anxiety, because at times, those seem like my selling points. At the end of the day, I have to question whether my list helps me find a husband or is actually keeping me from one.

Guarding our hearts "has been one of the most misused terms in Scripture," said Rachel, a thirty-year-old counseling graduate student, as she opened our conversation in Colorado Springs. "It doesn't mean putting up a wall or keeping people at arm's length. This has been an excuse and a way that we've destroyed intimacy. I'd venture to say Christian dating relationships are more unhealthy than regular dating relationships—and it's because we're trying to 'guard our hearts.'"

And to that I add: Why would this verse only ever be taken out and dusted off to be applied to a romantic context? Very rarely do we hear it even mentioned otherwise. Instead, we tattoo it on the forearm of every youth pastor (along with barbed wire around the bicep), and we make sure that those kids hear a sermon on it at least once a month. But what are we really teaching them?

Liz, a fellow writer who's been one of the biggest cheerleaders for my career (Thanks, Liz!), painted an experience very similar to mine, but she did it much more eloquently:

"This phrase made me a very snobbish high schooler, because all my friends were dating and breaking up and discovering they could survive that kind of pain. I wish I had discovered then too that I wasn't so frail so as to need such protection. I could have my heart hurt, and then I can pick myself up and twirl away. That would have been really good for me, because I didn't need what I thought I needed—I don't need to be wrapped in cotton."

Oh my goodness, yes. For so long, I "guarded my heart." I refused to develop relationships, even friendships, with boys because I knew that I was saving myself, because I wanted to be "relationally pure" for my husband. I didn't want to give away little bits of my heart to all these men and have them standing up there at the altar with me while I pledged the rest of my heart to my future husband.

I was naive. I was, therefore, ill equipped for college, a fertile landscape filled with desperate, prowling freshmen and unspoken expectations. The first time I fell in love, I was standing in line to get my car decal, and I locked eyes with the most beautiful boy I'd ever seen. He had the bluest eyes and patches of scruff that looked so mangy and manly it made me forget my name. I was infatuated. As providence would have it, we were in the same English class, and I knew what I had to do: capitalize on my strengths, offer homework help, edit papers, be funny (but not funnier than he was, obviously).

By the end of my sophomore year, my first unrequited love affair had run its course. But in that time, I was so irrationally attached to this boy I talked myself into all kinds of embarrassing things I now wish I could undo, like baking him approximately twenty-seven pounds of brownies and buying a guitar—that I said I already owned—so he could give me lessons. Needless to say, I still can't play a single chord.

After this crash course, I knew I needed remedial lessons on guarding my heart (and a refresher on how thick tank-top straps should be). Clearly all those youth group sermons weren't paying off. Here I was, spending time with this guy who had no intention of dating me, and, yes, it was incredibly painful. I was doing a horrible job of guarding my heart, and I came out of that experience with a serious question: How could I only spend time with men who wanted to marry me if they couldn't even begin to know they wanted to marry me unless I spent time with them? Yes, my friendship with this boy had never materialized into anything more, but it would never have had a chance if I had followed this youth group ideal of avoiding boys altogether who weren't ready to commit. The truth was, because I'd bought into this idea for so long, I wasn't prepared for how to develop healthy male relationships. And I'd easily fallen into an unhealthy one.

Alas, when everything you know about "guarding your heart" comes in the form of "avoid, don't attract, and flee temptation," you don't last very long at college. Enter Jake. Cue the same old destructive turn of events: fall hard and fast, pray for all my worth, still have feelings, resent myself and my feelings, develop deep insecurity, avoid him at all costs, return like a moth to a flame, and repeat this cycle for approximately five years.

The pain that comes from unrequited love is something that's pretty indescribable. And honestly, I've tried very hard not to describe it, because to fall in love with someone who doesn't desire you is humiliating. To fall in love with someone who sees and knows you and doesn't choose you is the very thing we all fear most. But, for some reason, this pain didn't change my course of action.

Because I'm a masochist, a few times throughout our years of friendship I had to tell him of my feelings, to see if he was interested (he wasn't). In one of our last interactions, I, emboldened by a hazelnut latte dusted with desperation, confessed everything one last time. Surely after five years of getting to know me, my love of young adult literature and propensity for undercooked brownies would have wooed him. In pretty explicit terms, he told me he didn't currently have feelings for me, he'd never had any feelings for me, and he didn't anticipate that ever changing. The immediate aftermath: two pints of cookie dough ice cream, one ruined shirt, one pillow that was de-stuffed in a fit of rage, and a broken light bulb (that one was an accident).

There's a special kind of shame in these situations, because if you never date a boy, you're not *really* entitled to heartbreak, right? I feel silly at times for even talking about him here. For all of you reading who've ever found yourself in heaving sobs on a shower floor due to unrequited love, I feel ya, sister. That *is* heartbreak. I remember many nights spent agonizing with God over why I was unable to guard my heart, why I couldn't shore up the defenses, circle the wagons, and pull out.

And to this day, I believe it's because that's not what we're called to do. We're not called to remove ourselves from pain. Those heartbreaks and tears and frustrations have taught me more about the love of God and the strength of my character than anything else I've experienced. Being hurt hurts, but it's not life-threatening, and the alternative can't be our only option.

"I had my first devastating heartbreak at twenty-seven, so at thirty I'm only now learning all these lessons I should have and could have learned at eighteen," Courtney told the Colorado group after I recounted a slightly less dramatized version of my own heartbreak. "I'm way behind on the bell curve of emotional and relational maturity."

And this, I feel, is an important point as well. If a boy didn't break my heart until I was twenty-four, it's no wonder I went off the rails (and ripped all the sheets off my bed and threw my mattress into the hall. It was a *rough* day). Liz spoke up to agree with us: "My girlfriends who were getting broken up with at sixteen learned at such an early age that heartbreak doesn't end your life."

My heart, I'm happy to report, is just fine. I still have much love to give, and I don't regret the years spent pining or the hours spent crying. The one thing I do regret is feeling so guilty for emotions I was helpless to change—convinced that by loving someone I knew I would never marry, I was less worthy of love myself. That by breaking off a piece of my heart and handing it to the boy, I was limiting the love I could give my husband and was capping the spiritual and emotional health I could achieve. I may have cried a lot over boys, but I'm better for it—not worse.

LIFE'S A PAIN

I understand why we push to guard our hearts, of course. Imagine how much pain I could have saved myself if I had been smart enough to avoid those relationships that didn't pan out. I know many other people in my life who would have been much more comfortable as well—because as much as we don't know how to sit in our pain, other people definitely don't know how to sit in it with us.

We try our hardest to save ourselves from pain altogether. Because if you're in pain, that means someone made a mistake—someone has to be wrong. Either you didn't guard your heart, or the other guy was a jerk, or life is cruel and unyielding. And maybe life can be cruel, but we are resilient. Like how a bone grows back stronger once it's broken, I feel stronger and better able to handle other difficult things in my life because my heart was used as a table to tap-dance on for several years.

Relational pain isn't the only pain you'll have to endure. You can get fired, lose a family member, or have a friend end a relationship, and all of these experiences build that pain muscle. There's no way to avoid it. And it's actually a wonderful thing, because then you can talk to others who are hurting. As 2 Corinthians 1:3–4 says, "Blessed be the God and Father of our Lord Jesus Christ, the Father of mercies and God of all comfort, who comforts us in all our affliction, so that we may be able to comfort those who are in any affliction, with the comfort with which we ourselves are comforted by God." We are comforted in our suffering so we can then comfort others—what a gift.

"My life has not been easy," Allie, a twentysomething medical recruiter, said as she shared a little bit of her story. "I've experienced the loss of multiple people. And I know I connect with people who've experienced pain. With my mom passing away three years ago, my brother is the only one who knows the exact loss. But even if you didn't lose your mom, if you lost a relationship or a job, you know pain too. Pain helps you be open to people, and it helps you love people better."

Going through pain makes us better able to love people who are in pain. I've wept with my girlfriends who've come home after a breakup. I've sat in silence with friends after they heard of a cancer diagnosis in their family. Am I secretly judging them for not guarding their hearts? Of course not. How could I ever chastise them for creating the deep emotional attachments we all desire? So why, then, do we do this to single people?

The problem comes when the church is removed from the pain of singleness. When the leaders don't get it. Instead of sitting in it with us, they offer trite phrases that only serve to aggravate the inflammation. They might use these pat answers so they don't have to really analyze and look at pain, but there has to be a better way to meet the needs of single people.

Let's leave room for lament, for mourning as the years pass and childbearing becomes more and more unlikely. As John Piper says, "Occasionally weep deeply over the life you hoped would be. Grieve the losses. Then wash your face. Trust God. And embrace the life you have."[3] Let's not berate ourselves for getting too attached to men who didn't work out or for being unable to tame our wild hearts. Instead, let's find strength in a community that encourages and equips us to use this pain to seek out God, to use this longing to relate to others who are seeking.

Undoubtedly you are terribly flawed, just like the rest of us. Your desires are wayward, and your attachments probably don't respond to stern lectures. But you are deeply loved. You are worthy of relationships just as you are. And there's redemption for all those years spent feeling guilty over a nonconforming heart. You're now in the club—all wild hearts are welcome here.

PART II

SEX AND OTHER STUMBLING BLOCKS

6

WHAT IS SEXUALITY?

(And Was Jesus Sexual?)

Sexuality. We hear the term *sexuality* thrown around quite a bit, but it's difficult to know exactly what it means. Is it referring to one's sexual orientation? To gender? Or to that magic switch that gets flipped on our wedding night so we can go from not thinking or talking about sex to being fully functioning sex goddesses in the time it takes to remove our dress and wriggle out of our Spanx?

And why is it important for single people to have a clear understanding of sexuality? Out of all my questions, this one, I think, is the most important. The answer? In short, an unhealthy relationship with one's sexuality can lead to destructive patterns that are carried into later single years or even marriage, as we'll talk about in chapter 8. And then there's the familiar shame that comes along with misunderstanding, ignoring, or suppressing it—a symptom of too small a view of sexuality. Additionally, when we accept and embrace our sexuality, we're honoring a gift from God. We shouldn't be embarrassed by our desire for both pleasure and connection. In fact, our sexuality is deeply woven into the makeup of our being, and, as such, it's running in the background of our system all the time, even outside of romantic encounters. So having a clear view of what exactly sexuality is and does gives us a better understanding of how it's contributing to who we are and how we're interacting with others.

In writing this book, I kept throwing around this term, *sexuality*, and eventually my editor very sweetly (in three or four or ten comments) said what you're probably thinking: *You need to tell us what this means*. And then I ran into a brick wall. Because what on earth is sexuality? I felt in my bones that the traditional thinking about it—the kind that limits it to the physical act of sex—was too confining; it felt like trying on a sweater that was three sizes too small. Sexuality can't be simply a special treat reserved only for married people, which is what the church seems to be saying when it only addresses sexuality in the context of sex itself. But I think it's so much bigger than that. It covers a whole, subtle aspect of who we are and how we relate to others, and I refuse to believe those of us who may never marry don't have this full human experience. I also biologically understand the implications of possessing a sex drive.

How would you define *sexuality* if given the chance? Some authors use it interchangeably with *sexual orientation*. Others use it to refer to a person's anatomy while never specifically limiting it to that sphere. And almost always, when discussing female sexuality, the conversation is stilted at best and evasive, vague, and shaming at worst.

But two Christian authors have recently attempted to shatter the mystique surrounding female sexuality. In fact, Dr. Kim Gaines Eckert, a licensed clinical psychologist, spent her entire book, *Things Your Mother Never Told You*, nuancing this idea. She has broken female sexuality down into four basic quadrants: biological, psychological, social, and behavioral.[1] She wrote, "I imagine the foundational building blocks of our sexuality as a Venn diagram of interlocking circles, which I will refer to as *body, mind, social identity* and *behavior*."[2] Eckert later described *body* to include biology, physiology, and hormones; *mind* to include cognitions and emotions; *social identity* to include femininity and masculinity; and *behavior* to include sexual activities.

Where Eckert's description of sexuality focuses internally, Debra Hirsch, author of *Redeeming Sex*, pivots externally: "Sexuality can be described as the deep desire and longing that drives us beyond ourselves in an attempt to connect with, to understand, that which is other than ourselves. Essentially, it is *a longing to know and be known by other people (on physical, emotional, psychological and spiritual levels)*."[3]

While these definitions are hardly complementary, or even compatible, I admire Eckert and Hirsch for puncturing the silence here. These two women are doing what many are choosing not to—they are bringing female sexuality to the forefront of conversation in the church, they are refusing to accept that female sexuality will work itself out in the vacuum it's been in for years, and they are working to provide it with a strong thoughtful and theological foundation. But unfortunately these ladies are in the stark minority.

THE CONE OF SILENCE

"There's no conversation about feminine sexuality in the church. It's too scary," Katelyn Beaty, former managing editor of *Christianity Today*, noted. "I will admit I've become a fan of the show *Sex and the City*, which is such a dumb show on so many levels, but here's what it does: it portrays women who are in their thirties who aren't miserable, and they're talking about sex. And as Christians we may complain that they're talking about sex outside of how God intended it, but at least they're talking about it. *Christianity Today* published a *Sex and the City* movie review, which we gave three stars for at least addressing this topic, and we had to take it down because people were so upset we had given it such a high rating."

This is the reality of the world in which we live. Out of fear or discomfort or shame, we in the church have relegated any discussion of sexuality to the act of marital sex. For years, I honestly believed my sexuality was something that would only be activated in marriage—just add rings! But now my desires and needs tell a different story. If the church isn't willing to engage in this discussion, if the only statement we'll provide is "Abstinence only, and then ask more questions once you're married," we're neglecting a large portion of the population, simply because we aren't comfortable or equipped to handle these topics.

Our conversations and theology around sexuality have to become more nuanced. They have to encompass more than physical intimacy, and they have to allow for people who are single well into their thirties, forties, or fifties, whether by choice or circumstance. Because God created us as sexual beings, and, as Dan Allender and Tremper Longman III have written in their groundbreaking work *God Loves Sex*, "sexuality is an integral part of the human experience. This statement is true of young and old, male and female—in short, of everyone who breathes."[4]

What does it mean that I, as a single, twentysomething female, was made as a sexual being? How does my sexuality manifest itself in my singleness? What does it mean for a married woman to be sexual, apart from her relationship with her husband?

Ultimately, what is sexuality? We need to build a solid foundation from which to talk about this. It shouldn't feel like a strange and foreign conversation, because there's nothing disgraceful or embarrassing here. Sexuality is a part of life, of each of our lives, and we can either take a deep breath and dive in and talk about it, or we can continue to perpetuate the silence. I choose the deep breath and diving in.

A WORKING DEFINITION

Acknowledging our sexuality means accepting that we are sexual beings from birth, from our very first moment. The problem is that our sexuality, like the rest of us, has been tainted by the brokenness of this world, by the fall of man. In response to this, the modern conservative church's rhetoric has emphasized what to avoid: exposed collarbones, meals alone with the opposite sex, mixed swimming, and the like. I understand the desire to cage it in, to rigidly define and control sexuality, so as not to provide room for error or sin. But as Romans 6:14 says, we don't live under the law—we live under grace. Does this give us a free pass to do whatever we'd like? Certainly not, but it does place the emphasis on *empowering* instead of *constraining*, which is consistent with the biblical model we see throughout the New Testament.

Before we can delve into what it looks like to empower rather than constrain, it's important for us to build a robust understanding of what sexuality encompasses. If we, as single people, have previously believed that sexuality was only reserved for romantic relationships and was therefore off-limits, we'll struggle with the shift in definition that says sexuality is something every person—man, woman, and child—cannot choose to deny and should, in fact, choose to foster. I don't advocate for this expanded definition lightly, but I do believe it'll be liberating for many. I recognize this view of sexuality will be entirely new to many of you, based on criteria that may seem foreign or even difficult to imagine. But I only ask that we continue to do what we've done so far in this book: have a conversation.

What I'd like us to consider here is but a working definition. I introduce it not as a shiny finished product but as a theory—one that, I hope, elevates the value of both singleness and sexuality and fits consistently with a biblical worldview and my own lived experiences. And it's evolving every day. But I felt like it was time to drag some of these ideas into the light, even if I ding them up and make them a little misshapen along the way. As we dive in, let's do so with grace and with the knowledge that what we've done up until this point hasn't been working. So here's an alternative.

Sexuality Involves Your Relationship with Your Body

Though many would limit their discussion of sexuality to the heavy hitters of biological sex, gender roles, and sexual orientation, I think it has a few more facets we must address, areas we wouldn't typically bring into this discussion. I believe sexuality also includes cultivating an awareness, ownership, and eventually an appreciation of one's body. Especially from a young age, it's vital we equip children with proper terminology to take full ownership of their bodies and, as a result, be able to identify assault or abuse more easily. This discussion is difficult for a few reasons. Obviously, people often feel embarrassed. They use made-up names for private parts in order to avoid any inappropriate conversations. But when a thirty-year-old woman still calls her genitalia a "muffin" and gets uncomfortable when she hears the word *vagina*, that's a problem.

Some may say using the anatomically correct names, like vagina, penis, and breasts, is unnecessary, that it's crude or obscene; but in calling sex "the birds and the bees" and in labeling sex organs with ridiculous names, we're implying that these things shouldn't be discussed. That good Christian people don't talk about such topics. I'm not ashamed of having a nose. It's simply a part of my body, and I learned its name early. No one insisted I call it a smelly-smelly. In using nicknames, we infantilize our own anatomy, further perpetuating the culture of silence around sex—and sexual abuse.[5]

There's a Harry Potter quote for every occasion, and this is no exception: "Fear of a name only increases fear of the thing itself."[6] Dumbledore's right, as always, and in this vein I choose to support the use of the correct terms. If this makes you uncomfortable, good. I hope you keep reading. I hope we all run into what makes us uncomfortable so we can grow in these areas. Acknowledging this part of our sexuality isn't easy—in fact, I'd say it's difficult most of the time—but it's so good for us.

And, perhaps most importantly, it's what the Lord demands of us in 1 Corinthians 6:19–20: "Or do you not know that your body is a temple of the Holy Spirit within you, whom you have from God? You are not your own, for you were bought with a price. So glorify God in your body." How in the world can we glorify God with parts we refuse to call by name? So that's exactly what sexuality aims to do—bring God glory with our bodies—and sometimes that's through something as simple as naming the body, clearly and without embarrassment. Maybe it also comes in emboldening children not to hug people they don't feel comfortable with because their bodies are their own. Or learning to love bodies that don't look the same, especially when that comes with self-acceptance.

As one woman at a roundtable said, "My sexuality teaches me to be comfortable in my body. If sexuality is suppressed, all my creative juices are suppressed. I've got to know that this body is safe and good, and not sinful, so that I can give out of a good place." She intuitively saw a connection between her body, her sexuality, and her creativity. Our bodies play a central role in our sexuality, and if we don't have a healthy relationship with them, that lack can affect so many parts of our lives.

Sexuality Involves Your Relationships with People

Another nontraditional facet of sexuality includes interacting with all genders in respectful and appropriate ways and seeking intimacy through relationships. This plays off of Hirsch's discussion of sexuality, so I want to loop back to her idea: "Sexuality can be described as the deep desire and longing that drives us beyond ourselves in an attempt to connect with, to understand, that which is other than ourselves. Essentially, it is *a longing to know and be known by other people (on physical, emotional, psychological and spiritual levels).*"[7]

I love that Hirsch's definition acknowledges this kind of interaction is by no means strictly *physical*, *romantic*, or *erotic*. Hirsch moves beyond these three descriptors, which most would assume must make up the entirety of sexuality. Intimacy, which is really what we're seeking here in longing to know and be known, can take many different forms, and that romantic, physical interaction is only one of them. So often, due to our shortsightedness and lack of nuance, we'll only be able to associate erotic or romantic interactions with our sexuality. And, honestly, I think we put ourselves in danger if we're only looking for those red flags before we identify a relationship as being tied to our sexuality.

Stay with me here. Let's say that sexuality is something much more broad, like interacting with people in respectful ways—acknowledging their boundaries and needs—and seeking intimacy through relationships—acknowledging your own boundaries and needs. Our sexuality affects each of our relationships, platonic or not, and theirs affects ours—even if we aren't necessarily "sexually interested" in each other.

When we don't acknowledge that sexuality plays a role in relationships outside of the standard heterosexual marriage, we feel exempt, and we set ourselves up for moral failure, secrecy, shame, and isolation. In fact, our intimacy with others and our community at large is also threatened by this false "sex-only" understanding of sexuality. When we understand that sexuality may not be inherently erotic or romantic and when we recognize that its undercurrents run through our relationships like a low hum, then we can begin to establish proper boundaries and communities that keep us vulnerable and honest instead of shrinking and hiding.

This is where we can serve one another, where the church can act as a source of support for us to come together to have honest discussion. This is also why I'm spending so much time talking about sexuality—because if we define it well, we can use it as a source for questions, for confession, for vulnerability, and for community building. Rather than letting our questions and issues with intimacy in relationships fester, we need to find a healthy way to approach the impact of sexuality in all our relationships. I am hopeful that we can love one another well in this. Church, this isn't a prescription but a plea.

Sexuality Involves Boundaries

People are drawn to one another—if you open my phone, the embarrassing number of social and dating apps will testify to this—but sexuality, as it empowers, also puts up boundaries. It says that we continue to talk about consent in sexual relationships because consent continues to be challenged. Because one in five women will be raped in their lifetimes. Because men continue to be sentenced to only a few months of community service once convicted for rape. We need to teach people how to be respectful and appropriate, because it's a part of our God-given sexuality. But the consent conversation doesn't start with the question, "Should you ever pressure someone for sex?" It starts at age three with, "This is your body. No one has the right to touch your body without your permission. And you don't have the right to touch anyone else's body without their permission."

Sexuality not only emphasizes the importance of community, healthy relationships, and consent, but it is committed to avoiding exploitative or manipulative relationships. We must put up boundaries, for instance, to protect ourselves from people we know will hurt us. Sometimes we choose to bring these people into our lives (boyfriends, friends, and projects, or people we try to fix), and sometimes they're the people who've brought us into the world. Regardless, with much prayer and godly counsel, we should not allow our emotional entanglements, unrequited love, or shared DNA to justify destructive relationships. As one roundtable participant said, "When I feel empowered in my sexuality, I also feel free to say *no* more. I become comfortable having those firm boundaries because I know what's acceptable. And I believe overall I'm less vulnerable to abusers."

And while we all examine our personal boundaries, it might be time for the church to start tearing down some of her own walls. Amena, a twenty-six-year-old VP of a nonprofit, said, "We can't turn off our sexuality, so if I just got some honesty from the church, it would be so much less shaming than silence." We're taught total avoidance: as a Christian, you can't talk about sex. You're not a sexual person. You don't get aroused. You're not sexually frustrated. We act as if these things aren't real until someone's in a relationship and we're defining hard lines and discussing pressures.

It's not that there are pastors preaching against hormones; it's that hormones and female porn use and high sex drives are never even mentioned. And once these conversations finally start, it doesn't seem like there are any answers. At a roundtable, Gina, the forty-one-year-old author of *One by One: Welcoming the Singles in Your Church*, noted, "The idea that there are older singles in the church who haven't had sex, it's kind of scary. We teach kids that sex is for marriage, but if you don't get married, we don't have another narrative available." We end up with all these singles struggling silently with no model of how to handle their sexuality in a healthy way. We've handed the conversation over to mainstream culture because of our avoidance, and faithful singles don't know where to go for an alternative narrative.

So it's time we create one. And we should start with Jesus, who was both single and sexual.

JESUS AS A SEXUAL BEING

"Do you think Jesus was ever turned on?" my friend asked me as we were in the midst of debating Jesus' sexuality, the odds of him experiencing physical attraction, and how he may have dealt with the inevitability of being aroused.

Honestly, it was in this conversation I felt closer to Jesus-the-man than I had in a while. Though the church may try to distance me from my sexuality, embracing this view of Jesus as a sexual being makes me feel like there isn't such a gulf between us. In being fully man (Heb. 2:5–18), Jesus had to navigate his way through sexuality as well—he had to figure out his body and control its reactions as a young boy and later as an adult, even as women knelt at his feet or tugged on his robes. He had to establish his boundaries, keeping unhealthy people far outside his inner sanctum as he tried to develop healthy rhythms. He cultivated intimacy with others, first with disciples and then with a select group of women, and in doing all of that, his sexuality was running in the background, just as ours does every day.

We don't like to think of Jesus as being sexual, though. Good Jesus. Kind Jesus. Even table-flipping Jesus. Those things are easy to digest and fit into our paradigms, but sexual Jesus doesn't come with a flannelgraph or Sunday school coloring page, perhaps in part because there are no verses directly discussing Jesus' sexuality. "I think most of us find it hard to think of Jesus as having sexual needs. Maybe because Jesus was sinless and we so easily associate sexuality with sin," wrote Debra Hirsch.[8] In our minds, the relationship is so close between the two—sexuality and sin—so to have a sexual Jesus is to have a Jesus who sins. And we all know that's impossible, so therefore Jesus must not be sexual. Problem solved. Let's go back to talking about the five loaves and two fishes.

But the link we've created between sexuality and sin is a man-made bridge. God created sexuality as a gift. It is a blessing to our lives, like creativity or intellect. Just because sexuality has resulted in sin doesn't mean sexuality is sinful. If we can start deconstructing this connection between sexuality and sin, we can remove some of the layers of shame in the church, and we can begin painting Jesus as the real sexual being he was. As Jim Cotter has written, "Jesus' sexuality was surely alive, however painful it may have been, however restrained in appropriate loving, but also a means of delight and pleasure shared, of creativity and union: to live such a life ourselves is surely not to be far from the Commonwealth of God."[9]

Here's why it's important for me to believe Jesus was sexual: I need to know that Jesus dealt with thoughts about sex, that he faced *every* temptation (Heb. 4:15), that he knew what it was like to burn from within, that he had his body betray him, that he was alone and did not want to be, and he was still without sin. I need to know that, in him, I can still find the picture I am supposed to reproduce, the model of human holiness I am to pursue, the original I am to replicate. As the Bible says in 1 Peter 1:16, "You shall be holy, for I am holy." I take comfort in this verse now, because in it I see Christ's commonality. While we didn't share a sin nature, we do share a human sexual nature, and in that he did experience much of what I find frustrating and isolating and harrowing at times. And it's comforting to know that he and Paul and Mother Teresa and Henri Nouwen and Richard Rohr have all gone before, have battled with their sexuality and, though they were celibate by choice or circumstance, they provide me a model of how beautiful it is when spirituality and sexuality combine—when two of God's gifts to his people work in tandem to the benefit of the kingdom.

There are no scriptures I can point to here to strengthen my argument, so all this is based on science, instinct, personal experience, and inferences throughout the rest of the Bible. There have been all sorts of wild claims throughout history regarding Jesus' sexuality, but this seems like a pretty basic one—it existed. I embrace my kinship with a sexual Jesus who also struggled against his flesh, against weariness and fatigue and temptation, and still he sinned not. That's a Jesus I actually admire a great deal, one I'm willing to spend the rest of my life trying to model both my singleness and sexuality after.

ANOTHER S-WORD

One more quick note: I'd like to discuss a practical way of looking at our sexuality as single people. Perhaps instead of viewing it as something to be suppressed or avoided, or something that's relegated only to the act of sex (because, as we've said, it's much more than that), we could view it as something to be *stewarded*.

The primary image my mind conjures when I hear the

word *stewardship* is finances. Money. Being wise in how I wield all my dollar bills. Stewardship is important whether you have a big fat savings account or a cute little checking account. No matter what you intend to do with that money or how you earned it, stewardship helps you learn how to manage all that's sitting in your possession.

Stewardship implies a cautious, responsible overseeing of something. I love to think of how that might apply to our sexuality: cautious and responsible. The purpose of stewarding money well isn't to gain power or influence, nor would that be the purpose of stewarding one's sexuality well, despite what some cultural accounts may argue.

Whether you are single or married, young or old, you have a call on your life to steward your sexuality well. To be wise and holy in how you wield it. To be intentional and responsible in the choices you make. This is what honoring one's sexuality, what healthy sexuality, can look like. Acknowledging sexuality in this way brings it out of the darkness and into the light. My sexuality is not inherently sinful. My desire to be desired is not sinful. Let's create a culture that respects and values sexuality, in all its different manifestations.

But, as with stewardship in other areas, I can make poor choices here. Instead of promoting healthy sexuality, I can use my sexuality to manipulate, I can become so crazed I make moral concessions, or I can refuse to learn what managing my sexuality looks like, and I'll yo-yo between repressing it completely or giving it free reign in my life.

This, unfortunately, is the state we currently find ourselves in. Because there's little room for this discussion in the church but there's little choice in ignoring biological needs, women have given up on meaningful conversations that unpack their experiences and have instead learned to compartmentalize anything having to do with sexuality. Our church communities should be places of safety and shared wisdom for walking the daily Christian life, but, unfortunately, when it comes to sexuality, they've been far from that.

As one woman confessed to me: "I went through a phase where, because I never discussed sexuality and never knew what to do with it, I engaged in some pretty self-destructive behaviors because I needed that outlet. But I didn't feel comfortable doing it in the church because I knew I would be shamed, so I went to bars and met guys there. That wasn't healthy either, but it felt, ironically, safer than trying to figure out this mess going on inside of me in a church culture where no one was talking about it."

I've heard other, similar stories. A friend who admits to a longstanding physical relationship with an acquaintance, others who find themselves in bed with strangers because the strength of the need overpowered their desire to resist. So many less-than-healthy choices born out of so much silence and confusion.

And once these choices are made, it's a downward spiral. Secrets can be easy to keep, for a time. And sin is pleasurable for a season. I had one friend compare her experience of a string of one-night stands to a champagne bottle finally being uncorked. There was so much pent-up frustration and curiosity and desire, that once she gave herself permission to indulge in this way, it took a long time for her to lose steam.

Friends, we can do better than this. We don't need to

be facing our temptations alone, sitting quietly in our unanswered questions, or ignoring this part of how we've been made. I believe there is a way to live unafraid of our bodies and also circumspect in our choices. There is a path to a healthy, holy sexuality, and we can find it together.

I'll leave you with a simple challenge: stewardship is never easy. This kind of holy sexuality requires constantly keeping a running tab on your account, on how things are growing and shrinking, on what needs monitoring. But stewardship is what keeps us healthy. Stewardship is the quiet, daily work of acknowledging your sexuality, seeing where it's integrated into your life, seeing where the edges are fraying, and being faithful to patch up as needed. So, for today, steward your sexuality. Maybe that looks like being especially attuned to a friendship that's growing in intimacy or to one that seems to be taking a destructive turn. Maybe you need to be evaluating your own relationship with your body (How comfortable are you? How much ownership do you feel over it?). Or maybe you just need to gently remind yourself, a few times, that after a lifetime of believing otherwise, you are allowed to be sexual.

See how it goes. And if you need to shore up a boundary or take one down, do it. If the reminder that Jesus was a sexual being brought you a bit of comfort today, maybe you could share it with someone else. If it freaked you out, figure out why. Let's start sowing seeds and see what happens.

7

MASTURBATION, PORN, AND OTHER BIG-TICKET ITEMS

When I first started talking about sexuality with a bunch of single women, I got the response you might be having right now. Lots of blushing. Lots of stammering. Lots of silence. But we pressed through that. We knew this topic was important, so we made ourselves lean into, not away from, what made us feel awkward. We eventually were able to go from discussing things in theory and sharing stories of "a friend of mine" to actually relaying our own personal struggles with lust and sexual sin and all that comes with that.

There's much fruit to be found in this process. Let's do the hard, tiresome work of cracking open this conversation. It's an act of grace for those around us, because we're all desperate for truth here, for empathy, for the knowledge we're not battling this thing alone.

And no, you're not alone. Whether you've never kissed

anyone and you're well into your thirties or you've done the one-night-stand thing and you're suffocating under guilt, you're not alone. Whether you feel like you have the sex drive of a teenage boy or you wonder if you're actually libido-less, you're not alone. Christian women who seek to please God fall all over these spectrums. You're in good company, but you'd never know it—unless we start talking about it.

Apart from being uncomfortable, all this stuff is tough to sort through because there's very little scripture that directly relates to the discussion of sexuality *and* singleness. Paul tells me to get married if I must due to my lust; well, Paul, if it were that easy, I'd have a minivan full of kids by now. From 1 Corinthians, I know I shouldn't think nasty thoughts about a man, and I probably shouldn't fornicate or become an adulteress. There's something in Leviticus about not being naked while on my period, and then Genesis promises me that childbirth will hurt like the dickens.

But everything else? The nitty-gritty discussion on taming a sex drive and learning how to embrace one's sexuality, that's not explicitly addressed in the Bible. Therefore, we can assume as long as we're modeling our discussion and choices on biblical principles this becomes a matter of deciding what's wise, not what's lawful.

Whitney described it well in our Lynchburg roundtable: "The opposite of encouraging shame isn't saying that everything is permissible. There are lots of things that we assume are sin that probably aren't sin, but we're foolish if we say there's no way for sin to enter this picture."

So how do I embrace my sexuality, even if I never have

sex? How do I know what's both permissible and profit-able? Honestly, I can't say for certain. So many questions are still floating around in my head, but I'm hoping that by sharing my own thoughts, and the thoughts of others, we can start working toward answers rather than being scared of the questions themselves.

THE *M*-WORD

Masturbation.

Oh, gosh, there it is. Right there on the page. I can only imagine the wide eyes and internal gasps many of you had reading that. In my discussions of sexuality, we always, always ended up here. More than twenty women told me this was their *first* conversation about masturbation. Ever. We're all pretty desperate to talk about it, because no one does. Well, at least women never talk about it.

I've been in Christian schools my whole life, from kinder-garten through graduate school. I've lived in the dorms and served on student leadership. I've diligently attended Sunday school and small groups. I've sat in church services a few times a week since birth. And I've never heard anyone publicly address female masturbation. But countless times I've heard male masturbation, male porn use, and the need for male accountability groups discussed at length.

That's because it's a man's problem, right?

Odds are, every woman holding this book under-stands that we struggle as well, but because the church is so confused on how to discuss female sexuality, and since the narrative is that this could only affect a small number of women, the topic isn't deemed worth addressing. The church has been remiss here, and I knew I couldn't write a book on singleness, much less singleness and sexuality, without discussing masturbation.

I remember the first time I was brainstorming this chapter out loud with an old roommate. Somehow we talked for thirty minutes without making eye contact once. (And then we may or may not have avoided each other for the rest of the day.) But as the year has passed and I've hosted round-tables where this was discussed, I've gotten much more comfortable, but I forget that some of the women I'm talking to are exactly where I was twelve months ago. So I'm absolutely giving you permission to feel freaked out right now. Do whatever you need to do—walk away, take some deep breaths, eat a burrito—whatever it is, do it, and then come back. Because we have to keep talking.

As with our sexuality discussion as a whole, there's no scripture to ground us here. There's an unlikely interpretation of an Old Testament story about Onan (Gen. 38:6–9), but that's the only real mention of masturbation in the whole Bible. Yet people hold such strong convictions on it. Immediately it's clear that at best we can only have a soft opinion either way. There's nothing biblically explicit to condone or condemn, and I would question the argument of anyone who came to this discussion with fire and vehemence. Now is the time for grace and charity, and I extend those to you and request them, because otherwise this could get pretty ugly.

I want you to read this entire chapter as descriptive—it's simply information for you to absorb. I can't determine if masturbation is right or wrong for you. Hopefully, in bringing some light to this, you'll at least be equipped to start thinking more meaningfully about your sexuality and how it plays out in your life and perhaps even discussing it with others (eye contact is optional).

"In order to talk about masturbation, you have to have that safe, vulnerable community. But it's hard to find that sometimes, especially in the church, which is where we're supposed to feel that most," Melinda shared with a group of complete strangers, mind you, at our Nashville roundtable. "It's not that the things we desire are bad things—it's that we want them so much it becomes a sin. It's not bad to *want* to have some sort of sexual release or orgasm, but it's finding some sort of way to deal with that. For me, masturbation isn't about a sexual release, but it's about how lonely I am. It's a way to distract myself from the fact that I'm alone."

Motivation is where this discussion has to start. Sabrina shared the thoughts she had when deciding whether masturbation was appropriate for her: "It's totally normal to long for companionship. But the guilt that people feel after masturbating, that's worth analyzing: *What are my intentions in doing this? What am I really looking for?*"

And this is where the thought processes come into play. As important as intentions are, I'm willing to bet there's not a single, straightforward motivation for most of us. There are many factors that deserve to be analyzed. A natural timetable every month dictates some of my desire, some is definitely fueled by what I'm watching or reading, and some comes in waves I can't predict or ignore. "Sexuality is always a multilayered, multidimensional story," wrote

Allender and Longman. "Our sexual desire begins with our first erotic impulses as we self-soothe by masturbating in the womb . . . The intrauterine child or newborn doesn't understand the concept or experience of masturbation; it is simply hardwired in us for relief."[1]

And then there's the relief, the self-soothing that masturbation offers. It feels good. It unwinds what's tightly wound. It releases what is pent-up. As a pastor friend of mine once said, "There's a reason God made your arm long enough to reach."

Could a healthy regimen of masturbation be part of stewarding your sexuality? Well, it depends on who you ask. This topic isn't avoided because it's uncomfortable; it's also a point of disagreement between many pastors, priests, and biblical scholars.

The correspondences of C. S. Lewis hold a bit of advice for us. In one of his letters published in *Yours, Jack*, he wrote:

> For me the real evil of masturbation would be that it takes an appetite which, in lawful use, leads the individual out of himself to complete (and correct) his own personality in that of another (and finally in children and even grand-children) and turns it back: sending the man back into the prison of himself, there to keep a harem of imaginary brides.
>
> And this harem, once admitted, works against his *ever* getting out and really uniting with a real woman. For the harem is always accessible, always subservient, calls for no sacrifice or adjustments, and can be endowed with erotic and psychological attractions which no real woman can rival.[2]

This objection makes sense to me. On more than one occasion I've blamed the stalemate of dating in the church on readily accessible porn. If men are being sexually satiated with their laptops, then that sexual craving isn't driving them to marriage (at a time when very little is actually driving us to marriage). And I've seen the wreckage of marriages that were created only for a man's sexual release—I wouldn't say either situation is ideal.

When it comes to this imaginary harem that Lewis mentions, though, I don't know that the illustration works for both genders. As much as I'll argue that women are just as sexual as men, especially if we're using the term *sexuality* in a more all-encompassing way, I will never say we're wired exactly the same way, nor is it fair to say all women are wired the same. So, if women are seeking physical release and relational intimacy, as I believe we are, masturbation is only meeting one of those needs—and even then, it's hardly being met. I imagine it's like a lion living off rabbit food.

Allender and Longman take a different stance than Lewis, though they address the use of imagination as well. They discuss the line between God-honoring masturbation and self-serving masturbation:

> The best way to enunciate the difference is to contrast a holy imagination with pornography. Pornography turns desire to lust as it makes one a voyeur of another's sexual activity . . . All masturbation that finds its core image centered on power, use, and degradation violates the true self-pleasure. It makes the heart small and cheap.
>
> On the other hand, masturbation that imagines the

man or woman who by character, generosity, and love—
let alone beauty and desire—arouses you is meant to stir
the body and heart to pleasure.[3]

Lewis's claims depend on the man desiring a submissive, readily available, attractive woman, who could be conjured in one's imagination. But if we're discussing a woman's desire for relational intimacy, that's much harder to imagine. As Allender and Longman noted, it is the quality of what's being imagined that's most important. If your fantasies aren't of control and power but rather of beauty and selflessness, as we would hope all sexual unions would be, then masturbation acts only to temporarily assuage a need without diminishing one's desire for relationship.

Just for a moment, let's take a more serious look at Allender and Longman's argument and imagine that there is a holy way to masturbate. Would that change your spiritual walk? A friend once told me that when she was single it wasn't out of the ordinary for her to pray before or after masturbation, consecrating the act and giving it to God. She believed that he gave her this body and this sexual desire and agency in this situation, so she wanted to satisfy the need in a way that honored him. I have other friends who've told me it's impossible for them to masturbate without going to places in their minds that they know are sinful, that they know aren't honoring to God. There is no clear path to right or wrong here. It would be easier if there was, but there's not, so let's walk, slowly, through this together.

Tara Owens brings good balance to this topic:

A single woman in her twenties who is discovering her body and her desires might be approaching masturbation as a celebration of sexuality and the gift of her body and desires; she could equally begin using masturbation as a place to take her sorrows, longings, and insecurities. In the former, masturbation can be a healthy expression of sexuality if kept squarely in the context of a relationship which, in her case, is with God, with her future mate, and with herself. In the latter, masturbation quickly becomes a place to go to hide from others and God, a place that, like any appetite-fulfilling activity, can quickly lead to addiction. Ultimately, the question of whether or not masturbation is healthy for a particular person springs from the question that governs all good discernment: *Does this action help me love myself and others more fully and freely, and does it allow me to love God more deeply and with more of myself?*[4]

If ever there was a time where I cling to 1 Corinthians 6:12, it would be in this moment in the discussion: "'I have the right to do anything,' you say—but not everything is beneficial. 'I have the right to do anything'—but I will not be mastered by anything" (NIV). Our bodies are so easily mastered, by foods that taste good, by routines that lull us, and by substances that distract and delight. They're also mastered by pleasure—and masturbation feels good, which is one of the scariest parts of it. If something feels that good, it can't possibly be permissible. But is that really the case? How do we determine what is simply natural and permissible and what may be natural but not? And how do we deal with this physical need?

Rachel Held Evans asked experts to weigh in on each side of the issue, and Abigail Rine, who teaches literature and gender studies at George Fox University, wrote:

> For those who plan to wait until marriage to have sex, masturbation can be a healthy way of dealing with natural sexual desire while single. The expectation that young men and women should go ten or fifteen years or more beyond puberty without expressing their sexuality in any way—and then suddenly "turn it on" when married—is, I believe, completely unrealistic and potentially harmful. How can we expect people to embrace the sexual dimension of embodiment in marriage while pushing the message that touching certain parts of one's own body is inherently dirty and shameful?[5]

Even Dr. James Dobson, founder of the conservative Christian organization Focus on the Family, deals with the reality of sexual need. In *Preparing for Adolescence*, a book he wrote for parents of kids who are entering puberty, Dobson noted, "It is my *opinion* that masturbation is not much of an issue with God. It's a normal part of adolescence . . . and Jesus did not mention it in the Bible." To those who do masturbate, Dobson wrote, "You should not struggle with guilt over it."[6]

Dobson, who's earned a PhD in child psychology, expounds on these thoughts in a letter online.[7] In the post, he addresses a few concerns surrounding masturbation: First, there's a serious problem when masturbation "is associated with oppressive guilt from which the individual can't escape. The guilt has the potential to do considerable psychological and spiritual damage." In fact, Dobson argues that it's not masturbation that has turned countless people away from God, but rather it's the guilt they experience over their perceived inability to please God by resisting on this point.

Second, Dobson raises an idea that's important to emphasize now: "Masturbation might have harmful implications when it becomes extremely obsessive." This is fairly straightforward, and I appreciated Dobson's explanation: "[This] is more likely to occur when it has been understood by the individual to be 'forbidden fruit.' I believe the best way to prevent that kind of obsessive response is for adults not to emphasize or condemn it. . . . Attempting to suppress this act is one campaign that is destined to fail—so why wage it?"

But the issue is by no means settled. For every scholar or writer defending masturbation, there is a priest or author coming out against it. In response to C. S. Lewis's letter, Wesley Hill actually found Lewis's response lacking for those who find themselves facing a lifetime of celibacy. Lewis's argument depends on the inevitability of marriage, so what is the drive to abstain from masturbation if you're sure you'll never marry? Hill wrote:

> I would argue that masturbation—or lust more generally—harms the celibate person too, not because it may hinder a future marital union but because it can also harm *friendship*. If the celibate person, no less than the husband or wife, is called to *go out of himself* in the love of friendship and siblinghood and in other bonds of kinship, then he also should want to guard his heart from constructing self-serving fantasies that have nothing to do with self-*giving*.

Moreover, if part of the rationale of Christian celibacy is to witness to the goodness of *marriage* precisely by refraining from sexual relations outside of marriage, then the sexual purity of the celibate—again, no less than that of the married—points to the beauty of a real man uniting with a real woman. ("By abstaining from temporary liaisons, the chaste and single reinforce the logic of marriage," says my friend Chris Roberts.) Therefore, even if Lewis himself doesn't spell this out, I can take his rationale for a soon-to-be-married person's chastity as relevant for my vocational-celibate chastity, too.[8]

Seconding this idea, Anna Broadway, author of *Sexless in the City*, wrote:

It's hard to escape the conclusion that the primary purpose of sex is profoundly relational: it's meant to tightly unify husband and wife in a profound, material metaphor of the self-giving love shared within the Trinity. So when it comes to masturbation, I have had to conclude that it falls short of God's intention for human sexuality. In my randiest, loneliest moments, I can certainly wish for a different conviction, but even then, what I most desire is not the freedom to masturbate with a clear conscience, but to be married and near enough to that spouse to once again fumble our way through the best earthly picture we have of the Trinity's penultimate love.[9]

I provide all these opinions because it's helpful to see that wonderful, wise people who love Jesus have landed all over the map on this. You have a personal responsibility to suss out the issue for yourself. We're both single and sexual, and with that comes a certain amount of Christian liberty. Praise God! But beware, thinking of masturbation as a less-sinful version of extramarital sex keeps us from having a robust, nuanced conversation about what it actually is.

Regardless of where we end up in our thinking about this, we must not retreat and hide from the issue itself. When we do, we give it free rein from the start. When we can't even say *masturbation* out loud, we cut off all safeguards that come from accountability. I know it feels pretty scary to talk about this, especially if you're not sure where your friends stand on the issue. Or if your masturbation habit has slipped from once a week to once a day. Or if it's gone from a masturbation habit into a porn habit. I understand. But if we can cultivate a community of accountability and vulnerability in the church, and if we can set up boundaries for ourselves, we can seek to honor God with our lives and our bodies, regardless of our views on masturbation.

THE SLOW FADE

A related topic but one rarely discussed in Christian circles is female porn usage. But the truth is it's on the climb, and with incognito browsers, late-night loneliness, and closed doors after 10:00 p.m., it's no wonder. As a love child of AOL and dial-up Internet, I am not surprised. I was raised online—I landed in chat rooms at thirteen and took part in conversations that started shaking loose the sweet, naive sentiments I held dear. I read fan fiction that would've made my brother blush. I learned how to write by LiveJournaling, and I learned how to take a selfie by MySpacing. I stumbled on porn by complete accident in sixth grade when I was talking with my friend jdrums16 on AIM and looking up something in a search tab. It was a pop-up. I still remember my chest flushing and how embarrassed I was. I couldn't stop thinking about that image for weeks. It was humiliating and exciting.

Statistically, that timing is about right, if not a bit early. About 32 percent of women see porn before the age of twelve.[10] Porn has traditionally been the man's domain, but its usage is becoming much more common among women, perhaps because we don't have to waltz in and buy a magazine from a clerk. We can simply hide under the covers. According to new statistics from Barna, 56 percent of women twenty-five and under and 27 percent of women twenty-five-plus have sought out porn.[11] In fact, in the twenty-five-and-under group, 33 percent seek it out at least monthly.[12] So are young women twice as likely to watch porn as their aging counterparts? Well, maybe. Part of the jump in these numbers is due to the fact that teenagers and young adults have more exposure to the Internet and are more comfortable in that space, but I believe part of it is also that they're more likely to answer these questions honestly, whereas older women may not be.

Regardless, the numbers are rising for both groups, and we need to talk about it. We need to talk about it as a church, we need to talk about it at our conferences, we need to talk about it right here, right now—because that's what you do when you're sick. I prefaced the masturbation discussion by saying I felt like that topic was a matter of Christian liberty, and I didn't think we could trust anyone who had an emphatic opinion either way. Let me be clear here: Pornography is not a matter of Christian liberty. We can't trust anyone who *doesn't* have an emphatic opinion here. I don't say that to shame those of us who have used it in the past; I say it to orient the discussion to truth.

Even while you can believe masturbation is glorifying to God, we must acknowledge that it can and does lead to pornography usage. I've heard this storyline multiple times in the course of writing this book. I wish this weren't the case. But in acknowledging that masturbation can easily lead to porn, we can establish boundaries and accountability to keep this from happening. In denying the connection, we only continue to perpetuate it.

Second Timothy 2:22 reads, "So flee youthful passions and pursue righteousness, faith, love, and peace, along with those who call on the Lord from a pure heart." Y'all, we've gotta run. Flee! This reminds me so much of Joseph resisting the advances of Potiphar's wife in Genesis 39. The flesh is hungry, and there are many people (and pixels) willing and eager to satiate that thirst.

But we are charged with the responsibility for our own spiritual walks: Selflessly love other people. Don't commit adultery, even in your heart. Think on true, honorable, just, pure things. And, when you fail to do these, repent often. Second Peter 2:19 says, "They promise them freedom, but they themselves are slaves of corruption. For whatever overcomes a person, to that he is enslaved." Do not be overcome—overcome your sin. Break the cycle. Satan is pinning you in silence, banking on your humiliation for his continued success. Meanwhile, your brain is literally being warped by pornography, your heart is being changed, your ministry is being affected. As a Christian, I pray your sin may grieve you, but never believe it shuts you out from God or from those who love you. Seek them out.

HOW FAR IS TOO FAR?

And then there's the land in between. I remember making my list of hard lines I wouldn't cross before marriage and writing it, as suggested, in the back of my Bible, but instead of putting it in pen, I lightly scrawled it in pencil—because even in middle school I knew "Save first kiss for the altar" was a long shot, or so I prayed.

One needs only to spend a few weeks in a youth group to hear bits of the "how far is too far" discussion. Those standards of "only hold hands," or "kiss on the cheek after engagement" are necessary and good for high schoolers. But I don't know that they transcend the test of time. Are my lines the same now as they were at fifteen? No. Should they be? I don't think so, but I know some people do.

We talk a lot about lines in high school, but that's where the discussion ends. Apart from a few close friends confiding in me for accountability, I haven't had a lot of discussion about "Here's how far I feel comfortable going with my boyfriend of three years" or "I regretted this, but not this."

Rachel chimed in at the Colorado roundtable with her

perspective as a counseling student, "Making out is really important in a relationship because you have to build your levels of intimacy at the same time. If you're building your spiritual and emotional but neglecting your physical, things will be out of balance."

We've all seen these couples. They've yet to kiss, but they spend countless hours on the phone together. They stare into each other's eyes in a way that makes me want to leave the room, and they've delved pretty deep emotionally and even spiritually, but that physical part of the relationship is lagging behind. One of my friends whose relationship was very similar to this told me that once she was finally able to be intimate with her husband, it felt like playacting, because they were going from zero to sixty on the wedding night. They hadn't taken the time to build up all these steps beforehand. It felt like they were level-jumping. It felt so wrong to be doing these things with him, even though they were married.

This book can't teach you where your lines should go. I can't make that decision for you—I can barely make it for me. But I will say there are lots of options, and just because you've done something physically and experienced shame does not mean the boundary you crossed was a biblical one. Personally, as I began to consider physical boundaries and what was healthy and even holy, I had to work through what was shame-based and what was conviction-based—and very rarely were they the same (we'll get into this a bit more later).

But once we sort out our thoughts and standards, and once those are tested, we should definitely be sharing our victories and losses. And when other people are honest with us about theirs, we have to use every ounce of kindness we have. Let's make the church *the* place where we create avenues for having real conversations with plenty of grace— extending grace to those who are questioning, those who are confessing, and those who are willing to listen.

Too often, we're all so scared of coming off as less than pure that we stifle these discussions, and we allow our guilt to keep us from comparing notes. We downplay our physical relationships so we don't feel judged, and in the process, we allow silent judgment to settle over our listeners who've gone further than what we're willing to say aloud. In summary: this is yet another part of our sexuality we're figuring out.

"We need people we can talk to," Heather said at one of the roundtables. "I remember asking my sister how far she went before she was married, and that was the most candid conversation I've ever had about sex and sexuality. We need to be honest. I'm assuming everyone around me is making good decisions all the time, and then I assume I'm the only one messing up."

We have to allow ourselves to wade into those sticky conversations of "was your top on or off?" and "what do you do with your hands?" and "I came into the apartment, and you and your boyfriend were horizontal on the couch. What gives?" I have friends who saved kisses for the altar, and I currently have a friend who is fighting for all of her worth to stay a virgin until her wedding (thirty-four days!), and it is *really, really* hard. I have friends who have never kissed anyone, friends who live with their longtime boyfriends, and then there's me, a girl who messes up sometimes, but in general is pretty boring, despite my active imagination and questionable reading material. If we all were less afraid to air out our dirty laundry, maybe we'd realize it didn't smell as bad as we thought it did and we'd be able to then help one another move forward from our not-so-wise choices.

"And let's talk about how sex probably will happen," Rachel added to our list of must-have discussion topics for the church. "Teach us what you should do if and when it happens. We've decided abstinence is the only conversation we can have in the church, but this struggle goes far beyond teenage years."

A friend who works at a church once tried to describe the fear she experienced when she believed she was pregnant— the thoughts that ran through her mind, the fleeting consideration of abortion (despite being staunchly pro-life), the humiliation and heavy judgment she already felt, though she hadn't told a single soul—and she carried that for several weeks. After a blood test came back negative, she texted me: "There's no baby. But I understand so much more now. What are we going to do?" We can stick to our abstinence-only speech and avoid all conversation about how to make godly decisions after a line is crossed, choosing instead a false perfection over a fractured reality. Or we can cultivate an environment that allows for the broken, weary, and sinful to bring their baggage and be met at the door with understanding and grace, especially for those situations that fall outside the ideal we're all taught to strive for.

"After my divorce, not having someone there to meet my physical need has been the hardest part of being single now," Melanie told a group of us. "And my ex has put it on the table several times that we could be friends with benefits, and it's hard to turn it down. But I don't feel like I can say any of this to my Christian friends." In situations like these, we end up turning to those who will understand, our unsaved friends, and their advice is very rarely peppered with temperance and self-restraint.

Like my friends who married young will never understand my struggles as a single woman, I don't understand Melanie's struggles here—but I trust her that it's hard. I empathize and cry out in frustration with her. These needs won't overtake us, but I do think they're distracting. They're powerful. And they can take up space in our minds and hearts when they stay bottled up all the time.

In drawing our hard lines, I encourage us all to remain heavily involved in community and in our local churches. These are the people keeping us accountable, asking us uncomfortable questions. Because I know about my friend who struggles to overcome a history of sexual abuse, I pray for her on Mondays at noon when my phone reminds me. One friend and I regularly compare notes on how our hormones are raging, what kind of weird dreams we're having, and if we feel we need to hold confession in the middle of Starbucks. And whenever I talk to that other engaged friend, we pretty regularly discuss whether she and her fiancé have had sex—and if one day the answer is yes, we'll talk about that too, just like we discussed how they crossed several of the lines they hadn't wanted to. It's not with guilt or fear; it's with love, because I want the best for my friends, and they want the best for me.

As women, we're not talking *about* enough: about what our bodies are doing, about how far we go with our boyfriends, about how we feel about masturbation. But we have to start this dialogue, and maybe it only takes one brave soul. Maybe it means you dog-ear this chapter and leave it open for your best friend to find, with some passages strategically highlighted and questions conveniently written in the margins. Maybe it means you start a secret Facebook group where people can start digitally digesting these topics, because I admit it's far easier to process my answers through my fingertips and a keyboard than it is through an in-person conversation. Maybe it means you simply start asking questions, good questions, because you love the women in your life too much to let them live in silence around these topics. Whatever it is, I'm proud of you, and I'm proud of all of us for continuing to wrestle with these issues, for not accepting the status quo, and for choosing to fight—for one another and for ourselves, even when it's not easy.

8

SEXUALITY ISN'T A SCIENCE

"I had to take a shower afterward." Recently returned from her honeymoon, my friend couldn't look me in the eye as she told me about her first time with her husband.

"Because it was messy?"

"No, because I felt so dirty. It's just . . . it's not what I expected."

This is how a two-hour conversation of hushed confessions began. As I listened, I learned my friend was shocked by her own emotional and physical reactions to finally having sex with her husband. They were the model couple—they did everything "right." They didn't kiss until they were engaged, they saved all versions of sex for the wedding night, and they spoke candidly about their fears and expectations. But then everything was so much more painful than she imagined it would be. And not only was it physically painful, she had to almost completely disassociate from the act of having sex with her husband to squelch the rising anxiety attack. She wasn't prepared for the mental and physical battle against herself. Having grown up under the teaching of fundamentalism, she understood that if she kept herself pure and abided by the guidelines being passed down, things would be perfect. *This* was far from perfect.

THE SHAMBLES WE'RE IN

The reality is that we live in broken bodies in a broken world; and no matter how tightly we try to control either of these variables, the brokenness will reveal itself in time, if for no other reason than to act as an ever-present reminder of the need for redemption.

It feels impossible to talk about sexuality and the church without diving into the discussion of shame and control and pain, especially as many of us are still healing up from purity culture and have the scars to prove it. For those who are unfamiliar, purity culture emphasized the importance of remaining physically and emotionally pure until marriage. Cultural relics like Joshua Harris's *I Kissed Dating Goodbye* and the True Love Waits campaign laid the foundation for the teachings in many youth groups.

Before going any further, it's important to acknowledge the value of sexual purity. As we talked about in the last chapter, there is a place for hard lines, and there is a clear call throughout Scripture to seek what is pure and good, to remain sanctified and set apart. I can point to verses that remind me it's not appropriate to go out and find a handsome man and have my wild way with him, even if that's what my body is begging me to do.[1] But it's important to note that even if I were to wear a chastity belt and throw away the key, the protection of my private parts does not guarantee sexual purity, nor does sexual purity guarantee spiritual depth and maturity.

This is where we often fall short in our attempt to hold to God's commands regarding purity. Our pursuit of holiness quickly becomes a letter-of-the-law striving when we're only seeking to modify behavior to meet a certain standard of purity, thinking that our hearts aren't in need of change. It reminds me of one of my favorite verses in Hosea: "I don't want your sacrifices—I want your love; I don't want your offerings—I want you to know me" (6:6 TLB). Our actions are our sacrifices, our lambs that we're willing to give to the Lord, but man, that matters so much less to him than our hearts. He wants our love, he wants to be loved, and he wants us to love one another. And that love will naturally produce sacrifice—it demands it. Sexual purity is a sacrifice, one that the Lord demands of us, and for good reason. Bits of heartache and relational shrapnel all over my interviews speak to the pain that comes from straying away from this command. This isn't arbitrary—it's what's best. And so we give it to him, lovingly, sacrificially.

So while it's important for us to consider our "hard lines" and to be prepared for our future relationships, I'm much more focused on our hearts here. And when we have hearts less concerned with walking with God and more concerned with merely exhibiting right behaviors, we fall prey to faulty ways of thinking. Eventually, we can start dispensing harmful if well-intentioned messages that overemphasize physical purity and underemphasize other heart-level growth, like cultivating kindness, advocating for the marginalized, or practicing mercy. And unfortunately this can do serious damage to the relational and emotional health of many people.

PURITY CULTURE, THE PRECURSOR TO SHAME

As I mentioned earlier, when I was in high school I took part in my own purity ring ceremony where I signed a virginity pledge and paid thirty-five dollars for a silver ring I promptly lost three days later (a bad omen for my virginity, to be sure). Almost all my friends were involved in this culture as well: we compared ring designs, discussed what we would permit physically (handholding is okay, but no kissing—which obviously leads to sex), and kept one another accountable by gossiping about how far other couples had gone.

Purity culture treats physical contact with the opposite sex in much the same way that eating disorders treat food. All contact is a threat. All contact can be sinful. All contact should be avoided at all costs. A hyperawareness finely attunes your skin to detect any possible grazing or touching. If you walk by and rustle my hair, I'm certain our courtship will begin soon, or so I believed in high school.

Perhaps unwittingly, these kinds of teachings actually heighten the sexual nature of touch. While friends of mine who went to public school and weren't heavily involved in youth group scoff at the idea of sitting through sermons that describe the evils of hugging, this was a regular part of my routine. The necessity of the A-frame hug—that's where your shoulders are allowed to touch the other person's, but none of the rest of your body should, as you both angle out like an *A*—was preached from the pulpit. When I took an informal poll on social media about who needed these hugs for self-restraint (so as not to come into contact with breasts or other body parts that could cause someone to stumble), it was my male friends from very conservative circles who admitted to appreciating the A-frame to avoid temptations.

It's interesting that the only men who confessed to stumbling over hugs were those who grew up in environments where hugging was seen as a threat. Perhaps in making a big deal about hugging, we were eroticizing something that wouldn't naturally be sexual. Did purity culture make purity more difficult?

THIS ISN'T A SCIENCE FAIR

What I experienced in the early 2000s with purity culture is indicative of a much larger problem: We, as people, keep trying to control sexuality. We try to make it simpler than it is. We try to pin it down and wrestle it into a label, a definition, or a series of descriptors that we deem appropriate. But sexuality isn't a science, and as much as we're scared to death by the uncertain nature of it (because it's totally terrifying), we can't allow fear to push us toward control, and that's what I saw in the purity movement.

In reaction to the sexual revolution of the seventies and eighties, the church was drawn to chastity, and in that crown, virginity sat as the shining, glimmering center jewel. I don't doubt the sincerity of the righteous zeal that spurred the church and drove them to fundamentalism. But the virginity being praised in youth groups was a fear-based metric, "used to divide the chaff from the wheat" (that was, unfortunately, a direct quote from a friend's youth pastor).

Virginity became the easy dividing line between good and bad, holy and unholy. Women especially felt this pressure to remain pure. While men were encouraged to be "good" in that they were disciplined and respectful, a "good girl" could only mean one thing: virginal. As a woman, you could be silly and vapid and dishonest and cruel, but if you were still physically pure, you were worthy of praise and esteem. It seemed that morality began and ended not with courage or selflessness or humility but with the hymen. "Virginity is the best gift you have to give your husband," I was told repeatedly. Growing up, it seemed the church elevated this single membrane to mean more than everything else in my spiritual life; virginity alone was indicative of the man I deserved and the person I was.

This view obviously lacks grace. Redemption. Hope. Virginity became a pedestal all of my friends and I were set on. One by one, as they fell off, I watched as girls would weep, trying to claw their way back up, knowing that they'd "fallen from grace." And all of the awful youth pastor metaphors only worked to reinforce this idea: If you've made compromises physically, you're a car that's been driven off the lot, and your value has immediately diminished. You're tape that's lost its stick, and you're going to be less able to accomplish your God-given purpose. You're toothpaste that's been squeezed out of the tube, unable to be put back in no matter how hard you try.

Sexuality is so complicated. In the fallout of purity culture, not only do we see a group of women struggling with their own virginity complexes, but we also see those who are unable to adjust to marriage—finding the transition more difficult than originally imagined. After years of suppressing sexual urges and viewing them as sinful, as opposed to God-given but untimely, some have confessed to being unable to quickly make the switch from "no, no, no" to "yes, yes, yes" after rings and vows were exchanged. A lifetime of denial and forced asexuality is difficult to reverse.

Others, like my friend in the beginning of this chapter, have to deal with fear and shame over physical intimacy with their husbands because the programming around purity runs so deep. One woman has to imagine the sex with her husband isn't consensual so she feels less guilty in the moment and is able to orgasm. If she can believe she's an unwilling participant, she can mentally allow herself to enjoy the sex more because she's not at fault—she's not choosing this thing that was off-limits for so many years.

Still other friends were met with serious disappointment upon learning that saving sex for marriage does not guarantee it will be easy or enjoyable. This was supposed to be the good reward, right? The medal at the end of the race. The victory lap we've earned for doing it all right. But very rarely is married sex immediately as easy or fulfilling as it's promised.

And then there are those who have lived with the reality of

prolonged singleness, who have developed unhealthy expectations and possibly even anger with God over the unfulfilled promises purity culture offered. Heather, who at forty-one has had to deal with this exact situation, discussed her experience: "For me, purity was about rules. When I hit thirty and was still single, it turned into being mad at God. I'd followed the rules, I did what he asked of me, I kept myself pure, but where had that gotten me? I did get involved in a sexual relationship, and it grew out of my anger at God. The bad part is that was a terrible reason to start that kind of relationship, but it gets so interwoven with the rules. These rules that if you follow them, God will bless you. And that's not true."

Simply put, sexuality is too complicated to standardize. It deserves more care and customization than a numbered list on a blog or a pastor's alliterated sermon. That's not to say that we shouldn't be talking about sexuality, but we shouldn't be talking about the one-size-fits-all model ("You'll both be virgins, so the honeymoon sex will be *great*. Neither of you should have much sexual baggage, so don't worry about that. Oh, and you two should have no problem having babies!"). Church, let's be willing to say, "You know what? Our lack of understanding about sexuality has led to a lot of mistakes. And we've hurt so many people, but we're willing to do better in the future. Let's start with opening up the dialogue today."

CHANGING THE CONVERSATION

Fear inevitably leads to control, and control breeds shame. For example, the husband who's fearful his wife is cheating will constantly seek to control her through monitoring her actions or interactions with others. This results in the wife experiencing extreme shame, even feeling embarrassed by perfectly innocent relationships.

In many ways, this is what the church has done: in a reaction against the sexual revolution and out of fear of unwanted babies or disease or regret, they've exerted great control. They've created a rule-bound morality that acts as a fail-safe against poor decision-making. Unfortunately, this legalism has resulted, inevitably, in shame.

I've said for a while now that you're only as sick as your secrets, so I daily attempt to live out vulnerability and forthrightness. To that end, I'll share my own experience with this shame. I heard it repeated a few other ways in my interviews, with different names and circumstances. Often it came with the request that if I told their story, that I please use it anonymously. Well, that feels like the kind of story that needs to be told. And I won't use mine anonymously, despite having reservations about releasing it into the world. This is my experience, and I have, even now, shame over it. I'm working through that. And since I know something similar is part of some of your stories, I'm happy to share it with you.

While I've never officially had a boyfriend, there was a boy I met last year. He's intelligent and bold and well-informed. After spending months talking online and on the phone, he came to visit. Three days later he broke up with me. Four days later I convinced him that was a horrible idea. Five days later he broke up with me again. (Seven months later, I know this was the right call.)

But somewhere in there, we kissed. A lot. And I

found myself struggling to connect with him physically. Objectively, I thought he was attractive, in a Prince Harry kind of way, but when we were kissing while the Alabama football game was on, I was more interested in the fourth-down conversions than in what we were doing.

But I had prepared for this! After twenty-seven years of self-denial, I was pure and chaste and ready to see what all the fuss was about. I was also petrified of kissing—not because I knew kissing would lead to sex, though of course I was unable to shake that assumption, but because . . . how do you kiss someone for the first time?

Most people get this mess out of the way in their awkward teenage years, and they can blame bumping teeth and uncomfortable hand placements on the innocence of youth. I, unfortunately, had no such experience. I did the only thing I knew: I watched YouTube videos. Hours of kissing tutorials. I considered practicing on strangers, so I made a Craigslist ad looking for a volunteer—and quickly deleted it (because that's beyond creepy, even for me). I interrogated my closest friends for tips and tricks. I, ever the overachiever, stocked gum, toothpaste, and breath strips in my purse.

As I knew it would, the kissing came, but so did an unexpected feeling of numbness. I was detached from the entire event. Now, not to make this weird, but I've always considered myself a fairly sexual person. I have a libido—and it's cranking along like an AC unit in summertime—and I've experienced the implications of desiring sex. But here I was, kissing a boy, all the while my body was completely unresponsive. After a few minutes (hours?) of this, I snuck off to the bathroom and called one of my best friends.

Whispering, I purged my soul of its one lingering concern: "I think I'm a lesbian."

"Well, that might be true. But why do you say that?" she responded, totally calm and unfazed.

"I'm kissing him, and I don't feel anything. The factory has shut down. The pipes aren't working. All the workers have called in sick. *I'm dead inside.*"

"Oh yeah, that doesn't mean anything. Sometimes when I'm kissing Colin, I'm writing a grocery list in my head."

Oh. Here was a biological reality I didn't understand before: kissing isn't always as it seems in movies. Sometimes kissing is just nice. There was nothing wrong or broken in me. And I accepted this explanation for a while—until I started sharing this experience and hearing from more women like me.

As it turns out, many women who grew up in purity culture struggle with this kind of numbness or detachment when getting physical. There's an inability to actually be in the moment. We've conditioned ourselves to suppress any kind of sexual response with another person, so in the act of kissing, intercourse, or anything in between, we can be completely unengaged.

Not only is it embarrassing to admit this to the public at large (sorry, Dad), but it also felt so frustrating. I'd finally found a boy I wanted to kiss and who wanted to kiss me, and my dang brain got in the way. And now not only do I feel a little crazy, I also struggle to not feel devalued as a result of it all. My first thought when he called things off with me was that I'm a less worthy option because I'd wasted these physical interactions on someone who's not my husband.

When it feels like the dating sphere is saturated with

lovely, amazing women who are successful and delightful and smell like peaches, any hit to my "amenities" makes me less valuable on the market, and that includes my physical purity. I didn't realize how much of my worth I was grounding in the fact that I had never kissed a boy. As frustrating as that was for me, it obviously was also a point of pride. So now, if I'm not as virginal and pure, I'm less likely to be married to a godly man—or at least these are the lies I told myself in the days following the breakup.

TEASING OUT SHAME FROM CONVICTION

For weeks after this experience, shame ate away at me. I was so embarrassed, so I lied to my friends about how far we'd gone, even though I didn't feel guilty about it. But I should, right? I didn't think we'd done anything wrong—I'd had some firm lines that we only brushed up against—but I still felt that familiar wave of shame wash over me.

Black-and-white answers are so tempting—innocent or guilty, homosexual or heterosexual, masturbation and porn are men's issues, not women's—but as we know, they do very little to actually advance the different conversations. Sexuality isn't easily reduced. It's complicated and messy, just like we are. And with it comes problems that are complicated and messy—namely, shame and guilt.

Anyone who was raised in the church, much less in purity culture, understands the power of shame and guilt and how often the two feel inexplicably bound together. Growing up I wasn't taught how to tell them apart, only

SEXUALITY ISN'T A SCIENCE

that if I felt bad about something, that was likely conviction and I should heed the Lord's tug on my heart, which usually ended with me throwing myself on the altar as the organ blared "I Surrender All." It was quite the spectacle. Through the years and through researching this book, more and more I've seen the confusion between the two, especially in areas that involve our sexuality. Eventually I began to notice a pattern: though I'd initially identify an emotion as conviction, I'd later be able to recognize it as shame.

To help us out, I want to provide a few definitions. Brené Brown, an expert in the field of vulnerability and shame, defines guilt as "I did something bad" and shame as "I am bad."[2] This is a sturdy framework for the discussion—and it's biblical. Second Corinthians 7:10 reads, "For godly grief produces a repentance that leads to salvation without regret." Godly grief, or guilt, or conviction—I'll use these interchangeably—will lead to repentance and leaves no regret or shame. True conviction, once seen through to repentance, doesn't require shame—sins are forgiven and you are turned away from them. Guilt exists to point us to Scripture, to help us seek out repentance. Shame exists to isolate us, to drive us toward separation.

I also appreciate Edward Welch's definition of shame in *Shame Interrupted*: "Shame is the deep sense that you are unacceptable because of something you did, something done to you, or something associated with you. You feel exposed and humiliated."[3] This explanation resonates with many who are healing from the shame they feel over sexual sin or sexual abuse or assault. These are scarring issues, and they find a way to seep down into the deepest parts of our bones—Welch's definition here gets to that. That shame feels all-encompassing of who we are. As Brown says, "If you put shame in a petri dish, it needs three things to grow exponentially: secrecy, silence, and judgment."[4] Shame swells in darkness, and the church has given it quite the playground by not bringing sexuality into the light.

What's frustrating about both guilt and shame is that they're only emotions—they are subjective feelings not bound to any objective standards. Even though we hope our guilt would be more in tune with biblical principles, in reality, a person's guilty feelings may not correspond with his or her actual moral standing. So, as we seek to sort through our feelings, let's ask ourselves whether they're pointing to thoughts of *I am wrong* or *I did wrong*. The first is shame, and the second is guilt. If you find yourself in the guilt category, that might not be bad. In fact, you might be experiencing genuine conviction (or it could be indigestion; this is how crazy the heart is). If you feel guilt, you need to ask if you've done something wrong—consult your actions and Scripture. If you're innocent, you can look at that guilty feeling, confront it with the truth, and work to move forward, repeating the truth as often as necessary. If you feel as if you are being called to repentance, repent. But then, as 2 Corinthians 7:10 says, repent and leave no regret.

THEN COMES SHAME

For those of us who struggle with shame, this feels like a totally different beast. I crave guilt, and I mean that earnestly.

Guilt feels productive—you weigh it, you measure it, then you either turn it into repentance or you discard it. Do not pass Go. Do not collect $200. For the shame sufferers of the world, we are envious.

Sexual shame is heavy. It feels like being buried alive underneath layers of secrets and stigma and contempt. And while everyone *out there* can talk about their sex lives and their problems, I feel like I can't—not with my Christian friends at least. And the damage is already done—the mistakes are made—so there's no hope in sight.

But thank God for redemption. Thank God for restoration and for forgiveness and for the fact that being abused doesn't mean you need to be forgiven. Thank God for people who listen without judgment and for conversations that have already begun, because that's where healing for shame is found: in conversation. In relationship. In realizing that you as a person are not what is wrong. In *The Soul of Shame*, Curt Thompson wrote, "Only in those instances when our shamed parts are known do they stand a chance to be redeemed. We can love God, love ourselves, or love others only to the degree that we are known by God and known by others."[5] I understand the fear here though. The instinct is to couch, to hide, to deny. But we all long to have the most broken parts of us be seen and held by someone and not to be found wanting.

What is our blueprint for seeking out healing and not allowing shame to rule our lives? Thompson continues:

Shame's healing encompasses the counterintuitive act of turning toward what we are most terrified of. We fear the shame that we will feel when we speak of that very shame. In some circumstances we anticipate this vulnerable exposure to be so great that it will be almost life threatening. But it is in the movement toward another, toward connection with someone who is safe, that we come to know life and freedom from this prison.[6]

It's what we've been doing all along in this book. It's what the very purpose of the roundtable represents. It's what Jesus in his ministry, as a single man, was able to embody: call out one another's most vulnerable and shameful parts, lay them bare, and still love one another. We see this modeled in John 4 when Jesus talks with the Samaritan woman at the well. It's a story we've all heard a million times, but as I read through it recently, after reading Thompson's book, I saw it with new eyes. Jesus came to the well and asked for a drink, and the woman asked how Jesus, a Jew, could ask this of a Samaritan woman. Jesus then told the woman of greater water than that in the well, living water that was greater than any she had ever known, giving eternal life. And here, at John 4:15, is where the story gets good:

> The woman said to him, "Sir, give me this water, so that I will not be thirsty or have to come here to draw water."
>
> Jesus said to her, "Go, call your husband, and come here."
>
> The woman answered him, "I have no husband."
>
> Jesus said to her, "You are right in saying, 'I have no husband'; for you have had five husbands, and the one you now have is not your husband. What you have said is true."

The woman said to him, "Sir, I perceive that you are a prophet." (vv. 15–19)

For the rest of the chapter, the Samaritan woman uses Jesus' knowledge of her as proof that he is who he says he is, but I also think that it does exactly what Thompson advocates. It's a Genesis 3 moment of God seeing you, seeking you, in your sin. We hide it because we know that in exposing it, in taking off those fig leaves, we are most vulnerable. But God seeks out those most vulnerable parts of us, as he did with the woman at the well, as he did with Adam and Eve, and as he does with you and me. He sees them, he calls them out by name, and he redeems them. He's died for them. For the bite of forbidden fruit, for the Samaritan woman's five husbands, for my sin and shame and for yours.

Kim Gaines Eckert wrote that "authentic sexuality should always make us more human, not less so. Sexuality should be connecting, not disconnecting. Sexuality is part and parcel of our whole selves; it is not just one part of us. We are ensouled bodies and embodied souls, and our sexuality matters."[7] There is nothing more connecting and authentic than being able to break down the walls of shame that enshrine so many of us. Just as Nehemiah called the Jews to rebuild the wall around Jerusalem by focusing on the bricks in front of their own lots,[8] I am calling us all to pull down the towers of shame in front of us, whether that's through sharing our stories with someone or writing a letter or finding a therapist. Whatever it is, do it. And when you're done, maybe help your neighbor.

PART III

HOPELESS DATING WITH HOPES FOR MARRIAGE

9

BAD DATING
ADVICE ABOUNDS

I've had sixteen first dates in a row.

About two years ago, I decided I was tired of wanting to be married but not really doing anything to pursue that end, so I joined several dating sites, started asking for blind-date recommendations, and followed one of the first (and worst) pieces of dating advice: give everyone a chance.

My first date was with Grant, whose profile stood out because of his incredibly unique interests, like drinking beer, watching football, and petting dogs. We talked on the phone for weeks before he asked me to dinner. As every good girl knows, I let him pick the place and gamely accepted my fate at a dimly-lit German restaurant. I scoped out the menu beforehand (advice I've been given: always be prepared on a date), arrived fifteen minutes early to position myself in the best lighting and in the best booth, and I waited with my hands shaking and my heart in my throat.

Grant was not impressed with me. Within five minutes, during which time he got me a drink I knew I wouldn't like (advice I've been given: let him order for you), it was clear our phone chemistry was more likely the result of shared loneliness than shared interest. Ever the engineer, he wanted to break down the chemical compounds in the drink, and I let him bore me to internal tears while I tried to imagine what he'd look like in thirty years (advice I've been given: look up a picture of his dad to see if you'd still be attracted to him once a receding hairline and slowing metabolism kick in).

Shortly after we ordered our meals, Grant tragically came down with a "stomachache," and asked the waitress to box our food in the kitchen and bring the check as quickly as possible. A check he requested we split, right down the middle.

Date two wasn't much better. It was a blind date set up by mutual friends. This time, I went in with different advice I was going to try out: Giggle, don't laugh. Let him take the lead in conversation so he knows I could be a pliable, submissive wife.

The date lasted approximately forty-seven minutes, during which time I did indeed giggle while I begged him to tell me more about his terribly interesting work at the tile plant, and I attempted to appear submissive, meaning I looked up at him through my eyelashes and smiled until my cheeks hurt.

He texted me that night to suggest we be friends. This one was actually a blessing because his car smelled like the inside of a rotting corpse. I still felt a tinge of disappointment.

In dates three through six, I adopted a new strategy. In

these rounds, I tried not to try too hard (advice I've been given: don't think about it too much, and don't seem over-eager). If I wanted to call and say I was looking forward to the date, I'd sit on my hands to keep from desperation dialing. If I wanted to make sure the place we were eating had food I'd like, I'd close down all my Internet browsers and instead maniacally color another page of my meditation coloring book. If, during the date, I wanted to actively engage in conversation, I made sure my face wasn't too expressive and my hand gestures were more Eeyore than Tigger.

I never heard from guys three through six again.

In my dates since then, I've ticked through all the advice I've been handed over the years:

- Go with your gut.
- Don't let your feelings dictate your relationships.
- Make yourself readily available.
- Don't be so needy.
- When you stop trying so hard, a guy will come along.
- You need to get out there and meet more people.
- Give up expectations of perfection—you're going to have to settle.
- Stop settling and going on dates with guys you're not interested in.

As I'm still single, and writing a book on singleness, and desperately trying to find that one *thing* that's off in me or in my dating so I can apply the magic fix and everything will be fabulous, obviously all of this bombed.

FROM BAD TO WORSE

At the end of the day, I don't know how anyone gets married.

Yet most of us do want to be married, and most people want us to be married, so bad dating advice abounds. It's everywhere—discussed at family dinners, whispered in church pews, and pontificated in online articles and dreadful dating books. I can't seem to get away from someone telling me this "tiny, little piece of advice" that will solve all my relational woes. And as Caitlin said in our Lynchburg roundtable, "So much of our advice is predicated on 'you're going to meet someone at twenty-two, date for six months, and then get married.'" Ladies, that's just not happening.

Singleness isn't the only thing people are trying to cure, of course. They hand out advice for parenting, job hunting, writing, and cooking, and ironically, much of the advice for finding a mate mirrors the advice given to those who are trying to conceive (advice I've been given: it'll happen when you least expect it!).

Some of the worst dating advice I've received, and that's been told to me in half-joking, half-crying asides, has my skin crawling:

"YOU ARE A DAUGHTER OF THE KING, SO WAIT FOR THE MAN WHO WILL TREAT YOU LIKE A PRINCESS." Contrary to all of the flashy memes floating around social media, I am not a princess waiting for her prince. In fact, I have a pretty large princess complex anyway—I don't need you to feed that. A man's life should not be built around taking care of me, and I shouldn't be seeking a man who will coddle and cajole. Instead of a prince, I'd like a partner—instead of someone who will pamper me, I need someone who will stare down the nastiest, most gruesome parts of life and not run for the hills. Also, it would be awesome if we could split things like nachos and ribs.

"IF YOU HAVE A PATTERN OF QUITTING RELATIONSHIPS, WHAT'S TO SAY YOU'RE NOT GOING TO QUIT YOUR MARRIAGE?" Oh, good gravy. This one acted as a serious deterrent for a friend of mine to end her relationship with a manipulative boyfriend because she thought she should "stick it out." Do not stick it out. Do not believe that your process of elimination in dating makes you some kind of divorcée-in-training. I've had to end multiple friendships for various reasons, but that doesn't make me ill-equipped to stay in tough relationships now. In fact, it's been a process that teaches me what's worth weathering. End bad relationships and stay in good ones.

"ATTRACTION CAN DEVELOP OVER TIME, SO IT'S OKAY TO DATE SOMEONE YOU'RE NOT ATTRACTED TO." I hope I'm not on the receiving end of someone practicing this advice. I hope I'm in a relationship with someone who sees me, is attracted to me, and wants to kiss my face off. And because I know I want that, I don't want to make the concession myself to date someone I don't find physically attractive, especially if we have a handful of dates under our belts. Also, there are multiple people who look like Ryan Gosling walking around this world. How could I pass that up?

"BE CONTENT WHERE YOU ARE, AND THEN GOD WILL BRING YOUR SPOUSE." Yeah, I don't think so. As Whitney said at one group, "God's not some trickster waiting for me to 'not want marriage' anymore." I've tried for a long time to not want something, just like every January 1 when I wake up trying to not want a chalupa from Taco Bell or peanut butter M&M's. And just like with my useless New Year's resolutions, the more I try and deprive and trick myself into not wanting something, the more it positions itself in the center of my brain. God's not looking for reverse psychology—he's looking for faithfulness and humility and love.

"FIND A GOOD MAN, AND STICK WITH HIM. LOVE AND ATTRACTION WILL COME." I'm guilty of saying this, and I honestly thought it was solid advice for all of us until my friend pointed out the problem here: "I believe a lot of Protestant churches fail in telling us to look beyond a checklist. I've been in an abusive relationship that looked amazing from the outside and he checked all the boxes. In the midst of the relationship, I thought the pain and frustration I experienced was simply him improving me. It was the sanctification process, because relationships are hard. But I wish there were more openness and intimacy so we can bring these real issues and say, 'He makes me feel like crap all the time. That's not healthy, right?' And the people who are giving me advice can look past his Bible reading discipline and theological opinions." Be in community with people who can tell you when the fears or fighting you're experiencing go beyond normal growing pains—and find a healthy community that actually knows the difference.

It's as if we're being trained to understand that marriage is "really, really hard," but we're not given anything beyond that. Why's it hard? And how hard is too hard? And when is "hard" actually "abuse"? I once had a close mentor who said something I still repeat to myself when I'm in the middle of a Twitter conversation about politics or social justice with yet another guy who is either trying to seduce me or fight with me (it's hard to tell): "We all have sharp edges—the question is do our edges dull each other or cut each other?"

ADVICE AT A HIGH PRICE

Some advice is silly or harmless, like when my grandmother insisted most of my troubles would go away if I only started kissing more boys. But some of this advice actually feeds destructive cycles, or it preys on our fears and weaknesses instead of driving us toward sanctification.

"DON'T MARRY SOMEONE WHO HAS STUDENT LOANS. IT COULD BE A RED FLAG THAT THEY'RE BAD WITH MONEY, AND IT COULD POINT TO IMMATURITY." I have student loans. I also have two degrees. And while I am a spender (as opposed to a saver), I'm not terrible with money. My ability to be a good wife and mother is not measured by the amount I owe to Sallie Mae. In fact, because of my ability to repay student loans, and even my outstanding balances, I'm building solid credit. I've learned how to budget in order to make those monthly payments. I've been surprisingly practical with large checks from tax refunds or Christmas presents—half to student loans, a quarter to savings, and a quarter to blow on going to see a movie by myself, complete with all the popcorn, soda, and candy fixins.

How could anyone know the circumstances surrounding my debt? When there are far larger issues to weigh when men consider wifin' up, how would this even make the list? And when did we start choosing a spouse that would give us the easiest, most cushy marriage in order to achieve that illustrious American dream?

By giving this advice, we're basically putting a dollar amount on a person's worth. How good does a person have to be to make up for how much they owe in student loans? I really love Jesus and help lead a small group, but I get sweaty walking to the mailbox and bite my nails when I'm nervous, so does that make me worth up to $20,000 in loans, but nothing more? In the olden days, women were evaluated based on their ability to haul two milk cans back and forth from the shed and muck out the horse stalls, because that's a woman who could help you run a farm and keep house. Now, instead of broad shoulders, it's a fat bank account (and trim waist). I prefer we throw out these vetting processes altogether. Marriage shouldn't be a matter of convenience.

"DON'T DATE SOMEONE WHO COMES FROM A BROKEN HOME OR STRUGGLES WITH MENTAL ILLNESS. THEY'RE GOING TO BRING THAT CYCLE OF SIN INTO YOUR MARRIAGE AND FAMILY." This one is painful. It cuts me to my core, because it exploits all of my deepest insecurities: I come from a broken home. I struggle with anxiety and depression. I fear, more than almost anything else, allowing these things to dictate the choices I make in my marriage. When I hear this advice, I can't help but think what a sad, limited view of grace and redemption it shows.

I am not irredeemable. The panic attack I had editing this chapter does not make me unfit to be a good wife and mother. My issues with food and body image and binge eating do not put a cap on how well I can contribute to my family. My traumatic childhood does not guarantee my failure.

I have to be careful—and honest—here. Because I come from a chaotic, unpredictable clan, I want to marry into a family that is strong and stable, where there are plenty of cousins for the kids to play with, sisters for me to bond with, and grandparents to guide us along the way. But this is not a deciding factor for me. I would never want to further victimize someone who grew up in trauma or someone who suffers from mental illness by deeming them unfit in this way. And any man who would dismiss me because of these things would have been eaten alive by my crazy family anyway.

"GO OUT WITH EVERY GUY WHO'S INTERESTED AT LEAST ONCE." It's a little harder to detect the harmful message in this one, because it sounds so reasonable ("Well sure, I can give him a chance. Why not?"). But here's what's at the core of a message like this: women are beholden to men to pursue them—our only agency comes in saying yes or no, and even then, we should probably say yes. So not only do I have to wait around until a guy sees how great it is that we could watch the hockey game and eat tacos together, but now I also have to accept a date with every guy who asks. I owe him that. Since a man expressed interest in me, I am indebted to him.

This plays out online more vocally and viscerally than in real life, but it happens nonetheless. Once, a guy sent me a message telling me I was pretty. I thanked him but told him I wasn't interested in pursuing anything with him. He said: "You're too fat anyway," and then he called me a name too awful to print in Christian publishing. And that was that. Courtesy seems to demand that I protect the male ego by accepting his advances (relational and physical), but I'm tired of playing that game. Like every man has the right to choose to pursue me or not pursue me, I have the right to welcome or rebuff those advances. I don't owe any man my time simply because he's interested in me, just as he doesn't owe me a date because our spheres intersect.

"FOLLOW YOUR HEART." The heart is desperately wicked. Whenever anyone tells me to follow my heart, I point that person in the direction of the door—because I've followed my heart, and I've come out looking like a fool. I followed my heart when I spent $112 on a guitar pick autographed by Led Zeppelin to give to the boy I loved who forgot he liked Led Zeppelin. I followed my heart when I wound up in the middle of Alabama, fleeing the sting of rejection over my unrequited feelings. This is terrible advice. Our hearts are foolish, fickle things. Making decisions based on them would be like buying a compass from the dollar store and attempting to hike Mount Kilimanjaro with it.

The problem with much of this advice so tenderheartedly administered is that it makes sense, kind of. If you squint your eyes and tilt your head to the left, you can maybe see how marrying someone who treats you like a princess really means you're marrying a kind man who won't leave you sniffling, sneezing, and coughing in bed, without medication or food, while he plays video games and eats crusty, leftover pizza.

I can also kind of understand that if you marry someone who has a pattern of cutting and running when things get serious, that could be a red flag. In theory, I agree we should perhaps be a little less superficial in choosing our dates.

But the problem with all of this dating advice is that

it's given prescriptively to the masses. The dating advice I needed at twenty-three, when I was in the throes of attaching myself to an unwilling man, much like Peter Pan trying to sew himself to his unruly shadow, was not "Make yourself more available" or "Be sure he knows you like him—men don't pick up on subtlety." It was, "Chill out, girl, and take the hint. Also, return that body glitter—it's not a good look for you."

And the advice my friend Jen needed when she was accepting a date a week with men she had no interest in was not, "Don't be so picky" or "You might just have to settle, within reason." It was, "Figure out what you want and need and be willing to wait for it."

If someone told me they were having marriage trouble, I would never start spouting platitudes and generic marriage advice without learning more about their specific situation, because I recognize that marriages are intricate, complex things, and the problems and solutions are as complicated as the people in the relationship. And yet we believe that passing out blanket advice to singles is going to fix our marriage stalemate. It's not that simple.

WHY IS DATING SO HARD? AN EXPLAINER

"Dating sucks," Shurti added in our Nashville roundtable. "It's basically a job interview. You're asking questions and determining compatibility. But if it doesn't work, you have to start all over again. It's so grating on your emotions. You get vulnerable and start building around a potential relationship, and when it doesn't work out, it's exhausting to have to start over and repeat this process over and over."

Dating does suck. It's awful and horrible, and it's one of the worst parts of being single. And what I hate about dating might not be what you hate about dating. Not all singles are struggling in the same way, and not all struggles can be fixed with a few clichés.

One of my favorite parts of doing the roundtables was listening to each woman describe the worst parts of dating for them. It made me realize how different we all are. Catalina opened up our discussion in Chicago: "I've enjoyed almost every part of singleness. But the hardest part is when there's a potential match—that anticipation or expectation that you might not be single anymore—and then having to adjust what your life might look like. Because I've spent so much time enjoying my singleness, I wonder if I'm even able to *not* be single. Is that going to be weird? Am I even going to enjoy it?"

This is not a conversation I've had with myself. While Catalina has to talk up the benefits of marriage, I continually have to remind myself that singleness isn't a death sentence. When a potential relationship doesn't work out, I'm always devastated. No matter how long we've been talking, I've already been mentally preparing myself that this could be my ticket to glory—to the promised land, and now I have to shift back to that place of contentment. But in order to feel motivated to continue dating, I have to be discontent enough with my life to want more. It's very hard to balance.

"Dating is also so time-consuming!" said Heather. "I just don't have time. And I feel this extra layer of complication because I'm a single mom. I want to marry a wonderful man, but he also has to be ready and willing to be a father of two boys. I was talking to this guy who was a pastor of a different denomination, and I wondered, *What will he be teaching my boys? And how will I deal with that when we disagree?* On top of that my sons are black boys, so I have the layer of wondering, *Is he on board with racial reconciliation and reinforcing the value of black men?* And if he's not involved in that world or thinks it's a bunch of mess, I can't be in a relationship with him. Since my boys are adopted, we also need to recognize that there's a difference there as well. It's a lot. I can't tell you the last time I went on a date."

If someone as lovely and articulate and intelligent as Heather has trouble navigating the dating world, in part because of her sons, that's a sad reality that probably can't be fixed with some trite advice.

Lindsley shared her own experience: "Dating after divorce is horrible. God bless those men I went out with. I would cry all the way home because I was like, *Is this really all there is out there?* I really do want the right guy to come—but I don't want to have to go through the process of sorting through them. I hate the dating scene. After divorce, you're experiencing this grief beyond belief, but you also have hope of what's out there. But dating sucks that hope from you, leaving you only with grief."

I don't think Lindsley's pain could be patched over with a simple "God will bring along the right guy" or "Don't date someone with baggage." God might not bring along the right guy, and we've all got baggage. We can't reduce the complexities of dating to a simple formula or list of dos and don'ts.

Once you're in a relationship, the bad dating advice

continues to come. Emily, our resident chemist, said, "I'm thirty-four, and as of today I've been going on dates with this boy for six months. It's the first time I've ever been in any sort of dating relationship, and there's a huge amount of pressure to define it. Our paths are very different, and he's not ready to officially label us. I feel really content with where this relationship is between me and this boy and God, but women in my life are putting so much pressure on us to label it, and it makes it so much harder."

When you look at someone like Emily, without knowing the details of her situation, you might say that she needs to pressure the man into making things official. You might say that at her age, guys are either willing to commit or they're not. You might give her bad advice that only works to aggravate her already-simmering insecurities.

In reality, these labels bring a false sense of commitment and security. We think that by labeling something the boy will be less likely to leave, that by getting him to commit to being in something official, there are better odds of it ending at the altar. This is a pressure cooker that will drain the life out from burgeoning relationships. We have to give things room to breathe. We have to give people space to make their own decisions. And we have to acknowledge that we might not have the answers for every situation.

I live in this tension of wanting to build a full, wonderful life that allows me to make hard decisions and live independently, a life that doesn't depend on the existence of a husband who may not come. I also don't want a life that's so full and independent it's impossible to add a husband to the mix. There's not blanket advice that will fix that.

So, let's stop. Let's stop trying to fix ourselves and one another, thinking if we try this one thing, we'll find a guy and then we'll get married and then all of our problems will be solved.

As Gina said in talking about this, "The one thing I wish someone had told me when I was younger was, 'Even if you don't get married, you'll be okay. I know you want marriage and kids, but no matter what, you're still going to be okay. You may have unmet desires, but life goes on.' That is a message that the church needs to be getting out there."

The success story here isn't the girl who wants to be married, and suddenly at age forty, as she follows all the advice she's ever been given, the stars align, she reaches a point of freakish contentment; then God deems it the right time, and suddenly she's married, rewarded for her years of faithfulness. Success in this world is the woman who lives her whole life longing for marriage, remains single, and dies more convinced than ever that God is good, with "Glory, glory, hallelujah" as the last words on her lips.

You're going to be okay. I'm going to be okay. Even though five minutes ago I took a break from writing to watch a video of two friends getting engaged, and I wept bitterly, with half a Twizzler in my mouth, because I want that. Some days I want that more than I want anything else (though getting this baby to be a bestseller is coming in as a close second). But I'm just fine. I'm happy-ish. I'm learning to kill bugs and make decisions and consider thinking about a 401(k). And it's good—it's a good life. And I won't let bad advice change that.

10

DATING IS A CESSPOOL, AND OTHER LESSONS

Do you remember in *Armageddon* when Billy Bob Thornton is mildly convinced that the entire world is going to end and there's no hope in saving it? That's kind of the way I feel about the dating scene right now. Tim Keller calls it a dating apocalypse. I like to think of it as a "Mating Armageddon"—both inside and outside the church. That's why, at twenty-nine-that-basically-rounds-up-to-thirty, I can be hopelessly alone on a Friday night, despite being willing to split the check, carry the conversation, and even indulge an anecdote about a pet rat. We've gotten this dating thing totally wrong.

In 1997, a twenty-one-year-old Joshua Harris kissed dating goodbye, and many in the church followed suit. Conservative Christianity raced to embrace not only a purity culture but also, in close tandem, a courtship culture, one that places pretty strict limitations on time spent alone with the opposite sex and encourages parental involvement throughout the process. While some of the more stringent observations have faded away over time, the essence of courtship still permeates the church.

Coffee dates have become interviews for the altar, and to say yes to a first date is to commit yourself for all of eternity—or so it feels.

YOUTH GROUP BATTLE SCARS

"The purpose of dating is marriage." I actively remember sitting at a conference and hearing the youth pastor, with thickly gelled hair and fervor in his eyes, say this with strong conviction. Heads nodded along, offering up their own silent amens (this was a conservative independent Baptist church, after all). These affirmations only spurred him on: "And I don't understand why our young people are dating folks that they can't see themselves marrying. It's a mystery to me. If you know that you want to head to the altar, you don't take a detour on purpose. You take the most direct route, and that means pursuing godly girls and godly guys who you can picture the rest of your life with."

I remember feverishly scrawling notes, hanging onto every word he said. After all, it sounds good, right? If there's a shortcut, you take it. If the purpose of dating is marriage, you only date people you can see yourself marrying. There's a lot that makes sense here, but the practical application of this philosophy has left me (and other wonderful, beautiful women like me) painfully single for the last two decades.

The problem isn't so much the concept of dating with purpose; the problem is the way this relatively sensible idea has resulted in fear and a tendency to hold people of the opposite sex at arm's length. We expect to be able to judge whether or not someone has Quality Spouse Potential based on surface interactions, because we're so scared of getting close, of "wasting" time and effort in investing in a relationship that then doesn't work out once we realize that candidate is no longer in the running. But this method is self-defeating. We're now putting only our best foot forward, concealing all flaws and weaknesses in order to appear supremely marriageable. No one is being themselves; we're all guessing at who will actually make for a good mate, and then we pray it all works out in the end.

In Chicago, Deb offered up more discussion on the worst parts of dating: "My church was that conservative evangelical community that, when two people in the youth group started dating, would ask, 'When's your wedding day?' So my entire adult life I've been programmed, and I'm trying to deprogram this thought process. If I go on one date with a guy, or even after a bit of flirting, if I'm not sure I can marry him, I panic and run in the opposite direction."

But, man, all that running makes you awfully tired. I try to stop myself from falling into this trap. Whenever I meet a guy who's about my age and we strike up a conversation (usually as I'm signing the receipt for the sub he's delivering to my apartment), I attempt to turn off the evaluators and scanners that are constantly running through my mind. Despite my best efforts, by the end of the conversation I've determined that while Logan has a great smile and is amiable enough, he's a bit short, doesn't share my sense of humor, and could never support a family on a delivery boy's pay.

How could I possibly know what Logan's true Spouse Potential is after such a brief interaction? I couldn't. But I act as though I can, and that's what's so dangerous. I pass up the opportunity to date Logan, or Robert, that sweet guy from grad school who I "don't mesh with," because it's not worth the risk of dating someone who probably, maybe, won't be my spouse, and it's not worth establishing relationships that will potentially only end in heartbreak instead of a honeymoon. But what have I lost in cutting off these potentials based on such quick, superficial judgments? Sometimes, I fear it's more than I realize. Here's what I've learned in the past decade of buying into the courting economy: remaining aloof until someone pledges undying love may be wise, but it's also a little cowardly.

"I don't deal well with loss," Jeanean said as she fiddled with her spoon and I sipped my coffee. "So I live in this tension of letting people in so they know I'm invested and I'm here for the long haul, but also holding back in case this isn't the long haul."

In my own experience, though, being guarded removes any need for self-reflection. I've recently thrown myself deep into the dating waters. While I'm a bit disappointed that I've been on a series of dates without even an offer of a second date, I know that I wouldn't have met a handful of those guys for breakfast again, no matter how delicious the pancakes were. But for a few of the others, their disinterest does cause me to pause, to ask tough questions about myself, my communication style, and my expectations. Though I haven't come to any strong conclusions, the process of questioning has been very beneficial for me. If I had continued to only embrace courtship, I never would have been forced into such uncomfortable, but ultimately profitable, self-examination. Because sometimes it's not them—it's me.

LOVE ME TINDER

The table is an ideal place for swapping dating horror stories, and in this culture, dating woes abound at our round-tables. With coffee cooling in our forgotten mugs, we laugh and groan in unison. This is what community is: coming together, in pain and frustration and weakness, to compare notes. To talk. To weep. And to feel less alone. That's why the image of the table is important to me, because you're not alone, no matter who you are, and your experiences and your dating horror stories and your heartbreaks, they deserve to be heard.

During our conversation in Chicago, Patty started ripping on online dating, which seems to be everyone's go-to these days. Since I'm an active member of six online dating platforms, all her frustrations make perfect sense to me. "How is it that I can sign up for eHarmony, only to find about thirty guys from my church on there, and then I've paid fifty dollars for you to ask me out online when I see you every Sunday?" Or worse, I've paid fifty dollars for you to have yet another avenue to reject me after I send you a saucy wink, as is usually the case for me.

And that's what I hear in these talks with women: we're all so tired. Tired of online dating. Tired of being asked about our relationship status. Tired of being set up. Tired of being set up with people who aren't interested. And some of us are tired of investing.

What all this weariness ultimately leads to, sadly, is a loss of hope. Katelyn touched on this idea: "When you're single and you've been single for a while, you really do start to think, *I don't know if this guy is out there.* I have friends who say, 'There's no harm in putting a profile up.' But there actually is a cost, and it's the cost of hope because of all the crazies out there who message you, guys who have poor communication and worse hygiene, and the harassment on certain websites. You feel really discouraged about the options."

If we're dating for the purpose of finding a spouse, then it's only going to work well one time. So yeah, there is some serious loss involved, and we can't ignore that cost. But we can't avoid it altogether, either.

One of my close friends, Jen, tells a story that's quickly become one of my favorites. A man with whom she had very little history recently asked her out on a date. As she nervously nibbled on a Panera salad, her date began to compare her to the Proverbs 31 woman and his own mother. Clearly, he was already sold.

Yet, while I love her very much, I can attest that Jen is not the Proverbs 31 woman. In fact, she's a normal woman, one who snoozes her alarm on accident and tells little lies about why she's late. She's human. And what's going to happen once her date realizes this unfortunate truth? Does her

162

worth diminish—or does her boyfriend grow dissatisfied—once her humanity begins to show?

When I asked her the hardest part of dating, Jen answered simply, "It's all hard. The whole thing. Sometimes I think that dating must be harder than marriage." And while I've only experienced half of that comparison, I think I agree with her.

MARRIAGEABLE: *YES* OR *NO*

I don't know if you feel this way, but one of my largest struggles is that now it seems people are only as valuable as they are marriageable. Some days it feels like once a guy knows you're not wife material, he decides you're not worth knowing at all.

It's hard enough when it feels as if this whole dating scene is a crazy, drawn-out game of musical chairs. In the beginning, when you're sixteen and carefree and only a little boy crazy, the game is still fun. But year after year, round after round, that music still plays and you see your friends scrambling a little faster to ensure they have a seat. You start to realize there are fewer and fewer chairs, and yet so many people. Suddenly your best friend since second grade elbows you in the ribs to get to a seat as the music screeches to a halt. And with all of that anxiety and pressure and sweating, the game's not as much fun as it used to be.

Dating is really exhausting. And when you have those days (and nights) where the difficulty catches up to you and you'd rather bury your head under a pillow, lounge in your leggings, and cancel on your latest blind date, know that you can join me for a *Golden Girls* marathon anytime. As long as you bring takeout.

I wonder if part of all this floundering is due to the fact that there's so much pressure to choose the *right* person. You have to feel that too, right? You have to search high and low to find that person who's a good fit for your strengths and weaknesses. That person whose life plan lines up with yours. That person who is patient enough and kind enough and spiritual enough. That person you've stopped calling the One but still secretly long to believe in.

Now, I love you, but if you believe this—this idea that God made you and another person as a perfect complement to each other—I need you right now to put this book down, take out a piece of paper, and list all the biblically sound reasons you believe the One or soul mates or other halves exist. Because here's what I know: God did not make us for each other. God made us for himself, for his glory, and for communion with him. The only *person* we were made for was Jesus Christ, and to give that position to any human is to elevate a bond far higher than it can sustain itself. That relationship will disappoint you. It will break your heart over and over again.

The One is a mirage we've constructed to romanticize the very real, sanctifying process of marriage, and it's hurting us, y'all. This idea is eating away at a true, beautiful view of marriage that has less to do with wooing and more to do with dying. Marriage is best seen in our weaknesses colliding with each other, not in us completing each other.

Isaiah 43:7 reads, "Bring all who claim me as their God,

for I have made them for my glory" (NLT). Did you catch that? *For I have made them for marriage* . . . Nope. *For I have made them for full, happy lives* . . . Nope. *For I have made them* for my glory. And this should be a comfort to us. You don't have to find the One or even happiness; you only have to glorify God.

But it's hard not to buy into this idea when people like Sheryl Sandberg, the COO of Facebook, say that the most significant career choice you'll make is who you marry.[1] Others word it differently but with no less pressure: whom you choose to marry is the most important decision you'll ever make.

That feels like a pretty heavy weight to carry on a first date, but we do it. Over and over again, I hear my friends (and, okay, myself) analyzing a dating or Facebook profile and discussing it in terms of "husband potential."

"He's got three part-time jobs. I mean, I'm glad that he's working, but where's the stability in that?"

"He spends a lot of time with his family. I love that. Being family oriented is really important."

"We couldn't fit a car seat in the back of a Camaro!"

You get the picture.

All this commentary, however, only highlights the fact that none of us knows what we're doing, do we? The pressure is too much. The stakes are too high. The thought of having to choose a partner who will help (or haunt) me for the rest of my life when my brain is barely fully developed? That's incomprehensible.

Consider that maybe you've embraced this courtship mentality because you're scared. Maybe you think, through overanalyzing, praying, and marriage-centered dating, you can actually take control of the situation. But you should know this method is self-defeating. In seeking the perfect relationship, you will eschew genuine, intimate relationships that develop as a result of grace, patience, and love being required and extended.

DATING AS CONSUMERS

Perhaps the advent of the Internet, and consequently dating sites and apps, has acted as a catalyst for one of your deepest fears as it has mine: there's always someone better out there. Are you picking the right person? What if you're settling, and then a better guy shows up in a year? Will this person be worth the sacrifice of your freedom? For women, these fears are only heightened by a race against the clock, an arbitrary expiration date that all good Christian women should be wed by or else lose the possibility of starting a family altogether.

When you browse dozens of profiles while wasting time on a Monday night, you see exactly how many people are out there. Instead of only being exposed to the three eligible bachelors in your small church, you have access to handsome, eligible bachelors from around the world! You may find yourself standing at the largest buffet known to woman, and with that empty plate in hand, you wade between rows and rows of options. Do you want the egg roll or the cheeseburger? The blond who can play guitar or the skinny youth pastor in Daytona? And as you reach to grab a pair of tongs, something tastier, better, catches your eye. Maybe you're like me, paralyzed by options and scared to death of choosing the wrong one.

But the truth is, when we only choose to engage in relationship with people who are sure things, with people who fit easily into our lives, with people who don't require work, we lose something. There is much to be gained in loving people who aren't the easiest to love. So as hard as dating is, it's worth it. And as much as it takes from you, it gives you something too: It gives you the opportunity to learn more about yourself and your needs. It gives you the chance to show God's love to another human being. It gives you affirmation that the less Axe spray used, the better. There are all kinds of gifts that come from dating.

We can't keep dating the way we have been, and we can't keep pretending we're going to meet a man and instantly know he's our future husband. (*Though, Jesus, I'm not putting limits up here. You can make that happen for me.*) So as hard as it is, and as messed up as we are, and as broken as the system seems, know that you're not alone in wading through this mess. And sometimes people meet right there in the middle of the muck. I've got a closet full of taffeta bridesmaid dresses to prove it.

11

MAYBE I AM TOO
INTIMIDATING

Do men avoid eye contact with you? Yes.

While on a date, do men make excuses to leave early? Yep.

In general, do men grow more competitive in a conversation with you? Sure.

Do they look away after you make a joke instead of laughing? All the time.

I was killing this. I'd always loved the quizzes in the back of those trashy magazines that sit by the register, and when I saw the topic, I knew I had to pay the $2.99 so I could take it (plus, there was a killer recipe for pizza rolls).

The results? *Congratulations! You intimidate men!*

Tell me something I don't know, *Cosmo.*

DEFINE YOUR TERMS

For a few years now the word *intimidating* has been bubbling to the surface of the dating sphere, but we're still pretty unclear as to what it means. In my Nashville roundtables, I had two groups of eight women each, and every single one raised her hand when I asked who had been told they were intimidating.

Sixteen out of sixteen yeses. That's a problem. And while interviewing women worked well for most of this book, I knew I wanted male input about what this label even meant.

"When men say you're intimidating, it means one of two things," my friend Stephen told me. "It either means he thinks you're too good for him or he thinks you're too much for him."

Too much. How many times have I heard that in my life? You're too emotional—too expressive—too loud—too opinionated. Too much. Yep, that sounds about right. And once I started asking others, everyone's definition of *intimidating* seemed to fall into these two categories.

"It's when a woman has confidence—when's she sure of herself."
"When a woman can control her social setting and she's in charge."
"She's really attractive, and she's got attractive friends."

Okay, so those don't sound too bad. If that's me, that's fine. I can work with "really attractive."

But then things took a turn for the worse as more men responded:

"It's used for women who don't seem to want to get married—they're too happy in their singleness."

"When a woman has accomplished more professionally or makes more money than I do."

"If she has opinions and she's not afraid to voice them, and not in a good way. She's bossy."

"A woman who doesn't try to make anyone like her."

"When I can't tell what interest level a woman has in me."

"She probably describes herself as 'too honest,' but in reality she's rude."

Right around this time, a guy I was kind of interested in had called me intimidating, so I pressed him, "What does that even mean?"

"It's like you're doing all of these things with your life. And you're terrifying. Impressive, but really scary."

I was even more surprised when I took this conversation to my friend Jake, whom I've known for years. I was telling him in an *Isn't this ridiculous? Let's make fun of him* way, but then Jake responded, "Oh yeah, I'm totally intimidated by you. If I ever wanted to date you, it's something I'd have to work through."

"But we've known each other for twenty years! You know me. You know none of this stuff matters to me."

"Yeah, that doesn't matter. You're still intimidating."

IT'S AN EPIDEMIC

As a nation, we've got women like Ruth Bader Ginsburg sitting on the Supreme Court. Michelle Obama leaving a legacy of grace and strength in the White House. Beth Moore, heroine in the flesh, acting as a powerhouse in the evangelical world with dozens of books and Bible studies, bestsellers many times over. And yet somehow we're still bound to the gender traditions that say men must be stronger, smarter, more powerful, and more successful than women, and this mentality is perhaps most prevalent in the church.

This is a message many women are receiving, from guys we're dating, from people in our small groups, from our well-meaning friends. When I brought up this topic at one of the roundtables, the air began to crackle. In a group of highly accomplished, articulate, intelligent females, this subject hits close to home, because for many of us, we feel as if we're being punished—or marriage is being withheld—because we chose to pursue our educations or careers, or we simply learned how to survive on our own.

In Nashville, Melinda added her experience: "Men are threatened by women who know themselves really well. Or sometimes they might be intimidated by women who have jobs and don't need a provider."

"It does seem like guys go for the damsel in distress," adds Jenny. "I was told flat-out by a guy that he wouldn't date a woman who owned her own home, because he wanted to come in and fill that role with and for her. If she was already that successful on her own, that was too intimidating for him."

Oh, good grief. I'm trying to be sympathetic here. I'm trying to be charitable in imagining how much pressure single men in our churches are under and how hard it must be to pursue women, but this is testing my empathy valve. When Jenny told this story, there was a general outcry at the table.

"What about all the money you could make together? Think about that, young man," chimes in Sabrina. "You could rent out that house. That's plain and simple insecurity. Men who don't feel secure and don't know themselves, they want someone who will boost their ego and tell them what they want to hear, instead of someone who will make them a better person. So, they go for little Sally, who, God bless her, she's a sweet girl. But she doesn't have much going for herself. And it might be purposeful—Sally might not have big goals and might be laying low. But it's going to be hard for somebody to grow in that marriage."

Women who don't need saving are certainly more firm in their own self-worth, they take pride in the work they do, and they will, as a result, rely on a man less. But while that may be intimidating, it's also healthy. The codependency found in the damsel–dashing prince relationships is hardly what we should be seeking to model. And yet, this is the kind of advice that's doled out.

"A few years ago my pastor was giving a sermon on singleness, and he said that the reason marriage was at a standstill was because women were too intimidating," Jaycelyn shared.

"He suggested we could—and we should—consider dumbing it down so guys would feel more comfortable approaching us."

As disgraceful as this advice is, I've gotten it on so many different occasions. When my dates don't go well, almost inevitably someone will suggest something similar to this: make the man feel smarter than you, make him feel like you need him, make him feel strong and capable.

Once, I went out on a brunch date with this guy I met

online. He was a thirty-one-year-old chemical engineer, and I was on a mission: I wanted him to ask me on another date. Partially because he looked like Clark Kent, and partially because I wanted to find something, some tactic, that would help me seal the deal to get these guys to call me back.

After we first sat down, we exchanged pleasantries, and I leafed awkwardly through the menu, pretending I didn't know what I wanted. Which of course I did—pancakes are clearly the best option—but I pursed my lips and furrowed my brow in a way that I hoped said, "I'm contemplative but not too bright." Once he decided on something, we put the menus down and began the typical interrogation: Where are you from? Tell me more about your work. What do you like to do for fun?

This man expressed a good deal of energy when discussing the power plant he helped manage, and he even teared up when telling me about his exciting work with uranium, his favorite element (and he was shocked and disappointed when *I* didn't have a favorite element). But I noticed when I spoke of my work as an editor or even the details of finally signing this book contract, his eyes kind of glazed over. I felt like maybe it was due to a lack of proper portrayal of information, so after he hijacked the conversation to tell me more about the use of lead pipes in his line of work, I circled back to this amazing book I get to write, and how I'm traveling the country to talk to women about it, and I used lots of hand gestures and had my crazy eyes out.

By the time I finished my sentence, he was literally asleep with his eyes open. For the remainder of the conversation, I deferred to him. "Yes, that does sound *very* interesting. So how does iron stack up to copper in this situation? Uh-huh, I can see that . . . I can't even imagine trying to handle that kind of thing on my own—you guys are kind of incredible to do that work."

By the end of the meal, the only additional personal detail I revealed was that I had poor grip strength, and please, kind sir, would you open up this bottle for me?

Clark seemed very happy with the progression of things. He even walked me to my car afterward. But you know what? He still didn't call me back—maybe his X-ray vision saw through my phony femininity.

Here's the thing about telling women their confidence and accomplishments are deterrents to finding a spouse: as opposed to empowering our men to find more purpose in a relationship outside of being the sole provider, we're telling women that they're the problem. This feels like a different version of the modesty discussion. It's not about equipping and challenging men—it's about teaching women how to compensate. We could be teaching that women are supposed to be strong, that intelligence is admirable, that ingenuity should be praised. But instead, we hear a sermon on women once a year on Mother's Day, and even then, it's probably extolling the virtues of only gentleness and humility all while lauding the accomplishment of mothers.

What's worse is we're actually allowing men to be much more multidimensional than women. You could be one of those big, gruff guys, but you're a teddy bear. Or you could be a small guy—you're not taking up much real estate, but you're so nice and friendly. As Sabrina says, "But when it comes to women, we can only be one thing: Sweet. Meek.

Pliable. Quiet. You can never be someone who is bold, loud, excited, happy, and definitely not angry—you can never be an angry woman. *Intimidating* is a cop-out. It's lazy. The insecure man is the issue here—you never hear a secure man talk about intimidating women."

EVERY WOMAN'S FAVORITE THING: SUBMISSION

In a lot of ways, the problem with women being intimidating comes down to a misunderstanding of what it means for a man to lead a home. We hear these terms in the church—*headship* and *leadership*—but what do they mean, practically? And is a strong woman truly a threat to a man's ability to lead well?

Many people would say yes. I've had a few frank discussions with men who believe that intimidating women, strong women, are harder to reason with and harder to lead; they don't tend to submit well. But that line of thinking leads me to wonder what we believe about submission in general.

Jeanean said, "Somewhere along the way, it seems that submission means that a wife disappears. But God created women to be a helpmate. She can be a wife and a mother and still be *who she is*. She submits to a husband, *and* a husband submits in leadership. It sounds like the only person who has to die to themselves in a marriage is the wife. And that's not the gospel."

We see these kinds of implicit beliefs surface in the discussion about women having it all, a topic that Katelyn Beaty is only too eager to tackle with me (and she does a great job dissecting this further in her book *A Woman's Place*): "Even for couples who claim to be egalitarian, for a wife to go on a writing retreat for a week or take a job offer that means moving across the country, that's never going to happen. We haven't taught men what it means to be *for* your spouse's flourishing. I've heard this idea before: 'You have to be lower than me for me to feel secure as a man in the marriage. I have to feel like there's some kind of power dynamic.' But that's the fall. That's not biblical."

At the end of the day I wonder if it all stems from fear. I would feel surer of my decisions if I knew I were always the smartest person in the room. I could effortlessly lead a team if I were clearly the one in power, and I had more talent, experience, and confidence. But when I'm working with competent people who are better than I am at certain things (or most things), that's a challenge—a welcome one. Do I fear they will question my decisions or that I'll make the wrong decision? Sure, but should that stop me from hiring the best people? Absolutely not.

Any man who chooses his wife based on who he believes will bend most easily to his will isn't looking for a marriage partner but rather a parrot. If, in his insecurity, he'd prefer to live with a woman who will allow him to make mistakes rather than voice her own opinion (or have an opinion to voice), he is choosing a dictatorship, not a partnership.

"I've had people tell me, 'I don't know if there's a man out there who can handle you,'" Catalina said. "But it's God leading me into these callings that require leadership. Taking on these different roles doesn't make me less feminine. I'm being obedient to my calling. But in some cultures, by taking these leadership positions, I'm basically taking on a man's role. Following God's call on my life hasn't felt like I was betraying my womanhood, but it has felt like I was betraying conservative Christianity's idea of what it means to be a woman.

"People tell me that marriage is so great, and I'll make such a great wife *if I . . .* stop dyeing my hair blue. *If I* sit in one place. *If I'm* completely silent. *If I* stop expressing interest in a guy and by some miracle he still notices me. But you know what? Maybe I'm good the way I am. Maybe I'm okay being intimidating, because what's the other option?"

If the only way to erase how intimidating I am to men is by making less of myself, by choosing not to publish books that worm their way into my heart, by laughing a little quieter or expressing love a little less, what would that make me? I'd be a shell, a husk of myself, and all that effort just so I could make a man more comfortable around me. That's not a compromise I'm willing to make.

COMING TO TERMS WITH REALITY

"In those years between my two engagements, I had to come to the point of being okay dying alone rather than being with someone who doesn't actually want me as me," Katie said when we met up in Chicago. "I'm willing to take that gamble and fill my life with people and relationships and community, and if that doesn't produce a marriage, I'm okay. I don't want to couple myself with someone who is going to box me in. But I do feel like there's a place to say, 'Am I intimidating because I'm kind of awful and bossy?'

Because that needs some work of the Spirit. Intimidation can be something you need to work on, but then it might just be that he can't handle it."

Katie's got a point. We can't cross out every claim of intimidation to equate to weakness or insecurity in men. We might be part of the problem. We might be rude or lacking in empathy or impossible to challenge. But we also might be blameless here. It takes self-awareness, reflection, and honest friends to help us know.

If you decide it's not you, if you've taken stock of your attitude and the way the Spirit's working in you and the way you present yourself, and you believe you're probably not chasing away all the men and people in your life with a rude, off-putting facade, what then? Well, you keep on keepin' on, ladies. What other choice do we have?

"Many women have to go through that process of 'I'm not going to shrink myself down. I'm not going to lower my expectations. I'm not going to settle,'" Katelyn said. "Now, you may have to ask yourself if your standards are too high, but most of the women I know aren't asking for too much. They're asking for a partner in life who will see them and love them for who they are—and that's a bare minimum. But it reminds me of times in my own life when I've accepted what was there *because* it was there. This was my last shot, my last chance at getting married, so maybe I'm okay with this."

This conversation is so good for my soul. I have a scar on my heart from a boy. It was one of those friendships where we had prolonged stretches of time together. We had mutual friends. We liked the same things. Our time together was rich and full and enjoyable.

Well, let me rephrase; it was rich and full and enjoyable to the extent that I admired and fawned over and praised my friend and his accomplishments. And because I so appreciated his company, I played this game. I asked questions I knew the answer to. I allowed him to do things half as well as I could, and then I applauded his efforts. I built him up with my words and time and respect.

When I got tired of this—because it's very exhausting to pretend to be something you're not so someone else can be more comfortable—our friendship was lost. I was easiest to be in relationship with when I was small and tractable and predictable. When I didn't challenge or question. When we both executed our expected parts. He wanted the quieter, slighter version of myself.

And that's where I see God's sovereignty. I came to realize that when I pretend to be smaller and lesser, my muscles atrophy and I'm actually both smaller and lesser than I was before. I can't live that life. I can't make myself less so someone else feels like enough. My ambition, confidence, and sense of humor are not liabilities—they're assets. And it took me a long time to realize that in preferring me when I deferred to him, my friend was actually only drawn to what I could give him rather than who I was.

WHAT (SOME) WOMEN WANT

"With people getting married later, chances are that a woman will have her own career or something that she's really passionate about," Katelyn wrapped up. "Maybe she has taken up leadership roles in her church. And are Christian men okay with that? It breaks my heart to think that there are women who are holding themselves back because they don't want to intimidate a Christian man."

One of the major things missing in our churches is a healthy model of female leadership, resilience, and courage—and all these traits being praised as strengths rather than weaknesses. Let's use our words, sermon illustrations, and even the passages we preach from to teach the value of a strong woman, a capable woman, an intelligent woman, instead of only emphasizing the virtuous woman.

While we're at it, let's also completely throw out our preconceived ideas of what the other sex is or wants, and let's rebuild from the ground up.

"I think men may assume I don't want to be taken care of because I'm accomplished professionally and I'm an attorney and I've already done so much," Heather shares. "But I would love to be taken care of. I would love to stay home with the kids. And I would say twenty years ago that was totally what I wanted to do—but that doesn't pay the bills, so I've been pursuing opportunities and trying to use my talents as best I could."

Some single women aren't as career driven as people may assume. Some of us, like Heather, are doing what we have to do with the time we have. In my ideal world, I'd be living according to a color-coded calendar on the fridge, telling me which kid goes to which practice on the second Tuesday of the month. But that's not the life I have, so I'm doing the best I can now. I'm making much of the talents I've been handed.

Meghan, who is very wise in addition to being very beautiful, said this thing, and I can't shake how right she is: "Where there's a disconnect is that women are being empowered right now, and men aren't being equally empowered. So, they call these women intimidating, but really they aren't instilled with—or aren't finding—the confidence that we, as women, are. Men already had the pressure to grow up and provide for themselves. But in adulthood, after I realized that my desire for marriage wasn't getting fulfilled, I've had to learn how to take care of myself. Then the question becomes, how do we empower men?"

This is a solid question, and answering it would lay a strong foundation for churches to build on. I feel empowered by my culture and family to do the big, hard, scary things that stand in my way. I am proud to be strong, and I can't imagine being in a relationship with a man who would ask less of me. I want to strive, together, with someone who teaches me, someone who challenges me, someone who exposes me to ideas and opinions outside my own. I feel like the village that raised me instilled these things in me— and I'm so glad they did. I'm proud to be an intimidating woman, and I'll wait the rest of my life to be with a man who's proud of me too.

12

DON'T SPEND YOUR SINGLENESS PREPARING FOR MARRIAGE

A beloved mentor once gave me a spatula. It wasn't a particularly beautiful or notable spatula. In fact, it was completely forgettable, except for\ the note tied to the end: "Praying for you in your singleness. This time is so valuable as you prepare to be a wife and mother. Hopefully this will help."

Her words were meant to be an encouragement, especially given that I'd spent an hour with her the week before, crying over some fresh heartache. And the kindness of her gesture almost made up for the searing sting of her message. Is singleness only worth embracing as a training ground for marriage? Is the best use of my time learning how to cook and bake for a man who may not come? We've asked these questions before, but now I'm going to attempt to answer them.

The short answer: no.
The long answer is a bit more complicated.

THE CHURCH'S MARITAL DISTRACTION

My mentor's advice wasn't new, but this was the first time I truly began to question the idea that we should spend our singleness preparing for marriage. Many dating books are peppered with this advice, but is it biblical? Or does it only feed the idol of marriage we've created in the church?

My life, my significance, doesn't begin at the altar, and I wish I felt like the church acknowledged this truth. Instead, the church feels centered around marriage. The Christian market is saturated with marriage books, marriage workbooks, marriage workshops, marriage conferences, marriage articles, marriage sermon series, marriage seminars, and marriage devotionals.

Some may respond by saying this market is comparable to the number of married people who regularly attend church. But it might be a self-fulfilling prophecy. If your ministry is only ministering to married people because the majority of those who attend are married, you will never grow in the number of singles you attract (nor will you grow in empathy toward the singles in your church). A church that waits to minister to singles until there's a large percentage will never have to adjust their heavy emphasis on marriage; singles will leave long before then.

But still churches and conferences and books insist that marriage is the norm, that it is the desired, inevitable end, so it only makes sense to utilize your singleness as a tool to make you better in marriage. Instead of helping all people, much less singles, grow into Christlikeness and learn to love and know Christ more, we teach how to become better wives and mothers and husbands and fathers.

For a long time, I took this advice. I started trying to cook more, ordering those fancy boxes of food that have step-by-step directions and ingredients included. On my first go, I burned butter so badly I had to throw away the pan. By the end of my third box, I was microwaving most of the ingredients in a single bowl and eating while standing over the sink. Wife fail.

I've tried to lean more toward my other womanly strengths. I've perfected the art of scrubbing a bathtub and bought into the value of greeting cards. I also believe one's hospitality is directly proportional to the number of pillows on beds and couches, so whether you're plopping down to watch TV or turning in for the night, factor in at least four to five minutes to remove all additional pillows and throws. I've gotten really good at vacuuming in a way that keeps those lines in the carpet. I'll walk carefully for days to preserve that freshly cleaned look. I babysit my niece every chance I get, and I flood social media with her pictures, so everyone sees how wonderful I am with kids and how much she loves her auntie.

You see, I tried to be a better wife for years, and when that comes I'm going to be awesome. But I've kind of sucked at a lot of other stuff because I put so much effort into the hope of something that may never come to fruition.

"That's such a small view of what the Christian life is,"

Jenny says, referencing this idea that singleness is meant to prepare you for marriage. "It's telling you that your ultimate goal is to be a good wife and mother one day, but there's so much more to being a Christian woman and advancing the kingdom of God and being a part of the church. You shouldn't be growing in those skills to be a wife; you should be growing in them so you can serve the Lord. This lie is telling you that your strengths and skills are limited to your family, and they're not."

She's right—we all know she's right. Our focus is too narrow when we make these kinds of claims about singleness. It marginalizes those who don't feel a call toward marriage, those who choose celibacy, those healing after the death of a spouse or a divorce. How can we tell all single people everywhere that this time is only valuable if it's used to prepare you for something else?

"And what does it mean to be a wife?" Sabrina interjects after Jenny. "That looks different in every situation, depending on the couple. You don't know what your marriage will need. How can I prepare to be a mother and wife today? Love. Practice love now. We should be telling people, 'Use this time while you're single to become a better *person*. Get to know yourself—that way if you do get married, you don't have to spend years in your marriage trying to figure out who you are. That's one of the benefits of being older, with our eggs drying up as we speak. If we do get married in our thirties and forties, we're more confident. We've already resolved issues within ourselves. We have more patience because we know who we are."

I love this advice, and I wish it had been Sabrina telling me what my singleness should be used for all this time and not a married woman gifting me a spatula and stoking dreams that may never come true. We, especially as women, have forsaken the art of self-awareness in favor of submission. The messages we received said that we didn't need to know our own wants and needs—we only needed to cater to everyone else's. We didn't need to learn our communication styles or love languages—we simply needed to know how to love others well. But there's a great deal of power in coming to know yourself, to love yourself, to trust yourself. I miss so much of that if I spend time constantly noting the ways I'm not measuring up to traditional gender roles and expectations.

Jeanean jump-started our Chicago talk with this idea, and it's stuck with me for more than two years now: "All my cousins are married, my aunts are married, and my parents are married. That's what you do—you get married. I was never really groomed for singleness, so being single at twenty-eight doesn't even seem real at certain moments. It's not what I was prepped for; it's not what I envisioned. My whole life I've been taught certain things: this is how life will go, this is when you'll get married, this is how to be a wife and a mother. But no one ever taught me how to be a woman. My biggest struggle is knowing what womanhood looks like, what identity and completion look like, apart from this goal of marriage."

I still get chills reading that. My purpose is not waiting for me at the altar or inside a cradle. I need to learn how to live a life that's pleasing to God right now—I need to figure out what biblical womanhood looks like apart from these roles we fill.

WHAT DO YOU DO WITH A GOLDEN CALF?

Something that often keeps us from pursuing biblical womanhood, that reorients us toward this marriage and motherhood definition, is the perpetual assumption that marriage is the end goal, the greatest possible outcome, the only desired destination. We like to justify the church's pre-occupation with marriage by saying we're simply reacting to a culture that's devaluing the entire institution, but in the meantime, we've made an idol out of the very thing that's supposed to be sanctifying us. I have to be careful here—the single woman discussing the idol of marriage in the church can provoke some ire.

"Many people consider marriage more important than singleness," Jeanean continued at the roundtable. "God made Eve for Adam, and therefore, they don't see singleness as a divine purpose. Sometimes people will make you feel like your singleness is a problem, but they don't even really know why except someone made them feel like their single-ness was a problem."

This is the unfortunate reality in many churches. We elevate marriage and minimize the value of singleness. In fact, the only time someone even mentions singleness is a gift is when I confess my desire for marriage and restless-ness where I am. It's an entire concept that's forgotten until it needs to be dusted off and handed out for comfort or cen-sure. Instead of highlighting truth to consistently celebrate singleness as a valid, beautiful choice next to marriage, we use it to cut off complaining and placate those who voice their desires for marriage.

The idol of marriage is hurting singles in the church. Honestly, it's hard for me to even separate my own personal desire for marriage from the desire my culture and the church have grown in me. I was raised to want this thing, and it was the assumed course my life would take. It felt as though the alternatives—singleness and celibacy—were only for priests, nuns, and stodgy college professors.

This is where we see the idol most clearly—when we prefer marriage to any other status, relationship, or identity. Some of my single friends would trade in their careers and communities and even ministries in order to be married. This idol also complicates dating, because how could a flawed individual who makes me cry when we discuss politics or snaps at the waiter for undercooking his steak possibly contribute to my flourishing?

Tim Keller says it well in *The Meaning of Marriage:*

> Both men and women today see marriage not as a way of creating character and community but as a way to reach personal life goals. They are looking for a marriage partner who will "fulfill their emotional, sexual, and spiritual desires." And that creates an extreme idealism that in turn leads to a deep pessimism that you will ever find the right person to marry.[1]

This has been my experience. In the past few years I've developed a friendship with Mark. He is well-read and kind and loves college football. He's also a pastor, but the kind that smokes a pipe and drinks bourbon and swears a little (which is the only kind of pastor's wife I could be). We briefly entertained the idea of pursuing something romantically (and on my lonelier nights, I still drift back to the idea), but once this discussion began, something shifted in my mind. I became very critical of his use of smiley faces in text messages. I was annoyed by the way he pronounced certain words. And with him only being a half inch taller than I am, I became very protective of my heeled shoes, so obviously this could never work.

When Mark and I were only friends, I enjoyed his commentary, appreciated his insight, and was thankful for his friendship. But this man, this great guy that I said on many occasions any woman would be lucky to have, he didn't measure up to this ideal I had in my head. And with the dissolving of our romantic relationship, I was swallowed up with the certainty that I could never meet someone I didn't have to settle for. Idealism and pessimism, indeed.

But Keller's description of marriage thrills me and reminds me how far I have to go:

> Within this Christian vision for marriage, here's what it means to fall in love. It is to look at another person and get a glimpse of the person God is creating, and to say, "I see who God is making you, and it excites me! I want to be part of that. I want to partner with you and God in the journey you are taking to his throne. And when we get there, I will look at your magnificence and say, 'I always knew you could be like this. I got glimpses of it on earth, but now look at you!'"[2]

Reading that brings tears to my eyes, because it's something I want so badly. And sometimes in these moments, I am aware enough to see my idolatry. I see the way my heart desires this good thing more than it does the glory of God. I hear the whispered words in the back of my head, secretly tacked on as a postscript to every prayer: "Lord, please let me get married. And please don't come back before I get the chance to have good sex."

When I believe I'm less of a woman because I'm not a wife and mother, I have the idol of marriage in my life. When I can't express any genuine joy at the engagement of a close friend because jealousy eats away at congratulations, I see the idol at play. When I manipulate situations and people in order to orchestrate meetings or in an attempt to grow romantic feelings, I feel the idol's pull once again.

Abraham's faith in Genesis 22 has always been a mystery to me. Despite knowing God had vowed to make him the father of many nations, Abraham obediently followed God's command to sacrifice Isaac, his only son. I can only imagine what it took to climb that mountain, believing God was asking him to slaughter his flesh and blood and the only hope of fulfilling God's promises. And just as Abraham had his arms raised, ready to murder Isaac, an angel of the Lord cried out, "Abraham, Abraham!" Some scholars say the angel cried out twice, because Abraham, unaware of the interruption, was so intent on his task, so sure of his calling, so faithful to do what the Lord asked. Hebrews 11:19 tells us that Abraham never believed God would forsake his promises, that in demanding the sacrifice of Isaac's life, he could also raise him from the dead.

I am envious of this faith. Occasionally I feel the Lord asking if I could give up the dreams I have of marriage, of having a husband, of children who will outlive me and be my legacy. And sometimes I even try to climb that mountain, ready to prove my love for the Lord by giving up this future. I tie these dreams to the wood and raise my knife in a shaky hand. But if I'm honest, I hesitate. I'm always waiting for the angel of the Lord to stop me—and he'd only have to say my name once. Some days I find it difficult to believe the Lord would ask me to forfeit marriage and motherhood, days when I resent him for even making me wait, and those are days when I see the idol most clearly.

I try to fight it, though. I try to own my desire for marriage instead of repressing it, and this has helped me reorient myself with truth. Abraham wasn't asked to hate Isaac or to even desire to kill him; he was asked to be faithful in what the Lord had asked of him. I take the knife and instead chip away at the golden calf I've erected. Even if God never gives me a husband, he is faithful and good, and I repeat this to myself over and over as I try to tear down what I've built up.

MARRIAGE IS DIFFERENT—NOT BETTER

The idol of marriage weighs most heavily in my heart when I am overwhelmed with life, stressed with work, or feeling lonely in my community, because in those moments it's easy for me to believe that a husband would fix so many of my problems, that he would lighten the load I'm struggling to carry. And while there's some sprinkling of truth in this belief, as Catalina notes, there's a line between believing things would be *different* and believing it would be *better*.

And this distinction, of marriage being a better option than singleness, harms the health of the church.

"People who are married might feel like they have to view marriage as superior to singleness, not just different from singleness, because they feel like they have to justify their marriages," Morgan says. "But what if they rushed into their marriages? What if there were impure motives or they were responding to family pressure and now regret it? Or they have doubts regarding their own marriage?"

If I'm doubting I made the right choice, it's easier for me to make peace with myself if I can find the weaknesses in the other options I didn't take. When I was at Liberty University my first year, I wondered if I chose the wrong college (because when you shove three eighteen-year-olds into a small dorm room and make them share a sink, one is forced to cling to the cross). There was a smaller school in my home state that I was constantly drawn back to when things at LU weren't going well. In order to soothe my discontent, I would look up the other school online and criticize it in my mind: *Look how small that gymnasium is. Can you imagine showering in there? I bet that girl is being paid to smile.*

But here's the thing—we don't have to keep playing these roles. You don't have to break down singleness in order to feel good about marriage. I don't have to diminish the value of marriage in order to accept my single state. My happiness does not mitigate, or lessen, your happiness. And your identity is not a threat to my identity.

We don't have to keep parading around marriages as the ultimate good in order to justify our undue emphasis on them. And for all of our efforts here, marriages are still falling apart. Abuse is still occurring within Christian homes, and divorces are still taking place. It seems that our idolization of marriages has done little to actually help them.

I want to share an e-mail with you from a male friend of mine who is married. He wrote it to provide a glimpse into the struggles of married life, to cut out the marriage PR. I hope that by reading it you'll see what I see: that marriage comes with its own struggles. That marriage, like single-ness, is different. It's not better or worse; it's a choice that can be made, a path that can be chosen, that has its own bumps and knocks along the way. And once all the flash is stripped away, it can be filled with suffering too.

The simple fact is, many, many Christians are unhappy and frustrated and even despairing in their marriages. But because of hang-ups or fear of how they'll be viewed or financial reasons or just plain lying to themselves, they feel unable to do anything about it or get help for it. This makes it very difficult for them to create deeper relation-ships with single people, because it's hard for a single per-son to understand that specific type of despair.

Marriage can be very ugly because it can make you feel like it takes some of the best parts of yourself and stomps all over them. It can turn perfectly good days into terrible ones because of stresses that have nothing to do with you and make no sense to you. It swallows your time and energy and effort. It can block you from things you'd like to pursue, ideas you'd like to try, risks you'd like to take.

I share this with you because it's easy for singles to feel that they are on the outside looking in . . . lonely creatures peeking through the window into the warm, cozy lives of families. And that feeling is perfectly legitimate, because being intimately loved is certainly a wonderful thing, and it kills me that wonderful people like you aren't having that experience.

But I think the other side is that sometimes (often!) married people feel as if *they* are the ones inside looking out: at freedom, and at opportunities for a loving relationship, and at a much more actualized life. They feel trapped in constant arguments, incredibly boring routines, financial inflexibility, constant judgment, and little to no hope that things will change. When they meet an attractive member of the opposite sex, they can't spend time getting to know that person. When the opportunity for an adventure with friends comes up, it's very difficult to make it happen because of the needs of the family. When the church needs money or help or volunteers, often one spouse is willing but the other is not.

I share these things because too many singles I know are hung up on the idea that marriage will somehow be better. And for some people, it is. But for some it is not. For me it is significantly harder. I wish I had known more.

Not all marriages are rosy bright, and I so appreciated my friend's honesty in sharing this insight. As C. S. Lewis says, idols always break the hearts of their worshipers.[3] I'm not implying my friend is in this position because he worshiped his wife, but I am saying that marriage is hard enough already—why put even more pressure on that situation by setting it up for failure?

Perhaps the greatest rebuke to the idol of marriage is found in Luke 14:26: "If anyone comes to me and does not hate his own father and mother and wife and children and brothers and sisters, yes, and even his own life, he cannot be my disciple." We all appreciate the support of family, and those who are married love theirs very much, but we must comparatively hate them. We must love them less than we love Christ. Our joy in these relationships must pale in comparison to, must be completely consumed in, our love of God. That's what we're called to here.

When dedication to one's family is being praised from the pulpit as the highest virtue, we've missed something. And if we continue to emphasize saving and restoring marriages at the cost of ignoring or diminishing singleness, there will be very few marriages left to save.

GROW TOWARD CHRIST, NOT MARRIAGE

So how do we resist the pull toward preparing for marriage? How do we prioritize our personal growth over finding a groom? "Jesus gives us a sneak peek into biblical womanhood with the Mary and Martha situation," Doni shared with our group. "We have these two women, one is the one who knows how to bake and cook and clean, and she could run a house like nobody's business. And then we have Mary, who just wants to sit at the feet of Jesus. She wants to go to Bible study, wants to go to Bible school. And Jesus looks at the two of them, and he's like, 'Martha, you see this? Put down that broom, girl. Hang up that apron.'"

Moving toward marriage is not synonymous with moving toward Christ. Cultivating domestic skills and practicing my child-rearing on someone else's kids won't make me a stronger Christian. And, at the end of the day, that should be my only aim—to know and love Christ more and to share him with the world. So, maybe I don't need a spatula to do that.

And honestly, seeking after Christ will naturally translate to being an exceptional wife and mom. Because of my love for the Lord, I'll love my husband. And because I love my husband, I'm going to get on Google and figure out how to make that stupid chocolate cake he always talks about, and I'll practice (and fail) a few times, and then one night it'll be sitting on the counter, waiting for him. And he'll see it as the act of love it is—but it's a love that stems from my love for God. And he'll ignore the eggshell bits. Bless him.

The Amazon River, which runs more than four thousand miles, has numerous tributaries, or smaller rivers, that flow off the main source. In so many ways, I view my love for my husband and kids and everyone else like tributaries branching off my love for Christ. If I dam that main river, the others will dry up. And if I'm only feeding one of those tributaries, if I'm only investing in cultivating a love, home, and future for my husband, that will be the only river that grows. I have to be pouring everything I am, everything I have, into growing that main river, because that's where all the others feed from. That's the only way it works.

Jazzy seconded this idea. "If you seek Jesus, that is going to make you a better wife. It won't necessarily give you all those hard skills, but it should make you better. Period. It is truly said, 'Seek you first the kingdom of God; then all these things will be added unto you.'[4] We read that, we quote it, we misappropriate it, but it's true. And when we focus on being a better wife over being a better Christian, we put marriage before the kingdom."

When we become pursuers of God, we will make amazing wives. And mothers. And daughters. And friends. Because when we feed that main channel, all those tributaries will benefit.

13

DON'T WAIT FOR MARRIAGE

Four months. That's how long I ate Teflon in my eggs before I finally broke down and bought a pan that wasn't chipping off black flecks every time I used it.

I was trying to hold out. I was trying to keep eking by with my old Goodwill pans, because fancy pans are what you register for when you get married, along with pots and nice plates and silverware and a KitchenAid mixer and a Wii and a lava lamp. Why would I go out and buy nice stuff when I'm the only one using it?

Because I can. That's why.

If you haven't seen *Parks and Recreation*, you're missing out. One of my favorite parts of the whole show is the recurring holiday when the characters Donna and Tom decide it's time to "Treat Yo'self!" They splurge on clothes and perfume and massages and fine leather goods. It's wonderful to watch.

I wish more single women had this philosophy as well.

We put too much aside as we wait for marriage. There are the predictable things, like swanky pots and pans that we're unwilling (or unable) to spend a fortune on, but also experiences and trips and relationships we keep looking at and saying "not yet."

Well, why the heck not?

Despite the fact that I am five feet, ten inches tall, I slept on a twin mattress until I was twenty-seven. When I took a very adult job in Colorado, I sold all my furniture before I moved. When I got there, I had to furnish a two-bedroom apartment. It was the first time I had ever lived by myself, and it was the first time I didn't have to reconcile my Jack Vettriano prints with someone else's cheetah cushions as we merged our lives and possessions in order to split rent.

Decorating that apartment was one of the most fun (and expensive) things I've ever done. As it turns out, my style is "rustic, industrial comfort," which loosely translates to a humongous couch, wood and metal tables, and so many pillows.

As I picked out lamps and dining-room chairs and cutting boards, I realized that this privilege shouldn't be limited to the engaged or the married. I have a home, a place I want to feel warm and welcoming, even if the other side of the bed is empty, and that means I should invest in colorful curtains and mood lighting. And a decent-sized bed. I am happy to tell you I now sleep in a queen bed, and my feet don't hang off the end anymore. In fact, between the mattress topper and fancy sheets, my bed is one of my happy places.

I'll wait until I get married, and then I'll . . .

Buy a new car.
Travel the world.
Get a new vacuum.
Tithe more.
Join a small group.
Volunteer somewhere.
Start saving for retirement.

The list goes on and on. Unfortunately, the longer we're single, the more we could add to the list, because we seem to discover more and more things we're unable or uncomfortable doing by ourselves.

"You know what would be a game-changer?" asked Whitney at our Lynchburg roundtable. "If, from the time you were little girls, you're taught that God has an amazing life for you, and we don't know if that includes marriage and kids or not, but God is good and he has good things for you."

That message is everything I'm trying to say. We, as single women, will naturally bump up against some limitations: tax breaks we won't qualify for, discounts we can't receive, memories we won't be able to make. We can't, then, impose additional restrictions simply because it's culturally more acceptable to receive mixing bowls as a wedding gift than to buy them for ourselves.

But, like water building up behind a dam, eventually the dam breaks. And those women who've had enough—those women who are tired of waiting, tired of restraining dreams and hopes and aspirations for a marriage that may not come—those are my favorite people. They're frightening in their intensity, almost like they realize they've been living in a waiting room, depriving themselves of all this world has to offer.

I'm tired of expectations and cultural conditioning telling me what I can and cannot do. I am a single woman, and I will write a book. I am a single woman, and I can change my own car battery. I am a single woman, and I'm buying twelve place settings of china that are turquoise and orange (and they are *cute*).

You see, eventually I learned the more I deprived myself, the more I longed for marriage so I could have all these fab things I didn't believe I had the right to place in my Amazon cart. As if at checkout there would be a questionnaire: *Are you getting married? Do you really need twelve glasses? What if your future husband hates the shape of these bowls?*

Fear ultimately drove much of my hesitation. What if I buy all this stuff, and he hates it? What if I buy it, and I'm the only one to see it? What if it won't fit in our cute one-bedroom studio apartment because we're poor newlyweds?

But I grew tired of being afraid, grew tired of waiting for the good stuff. There's freedom in throwing off this mantle of waiting for marriage and reveling in the truth that you don't have to wait. Buy the pans. Do the big things. Travel to that place. Drink deeply of this life God has given you.

WHAT'S AT STAKE

"Buying a house. That's mine," Jenny responded when I asked a group of women what they were waiting on for marriage. "I keep going back and forth in my mind: it'd be nice to have a house, but it'd be better to do this with some-one else. The longer I'm single, the more sense it makes to buy, but that's hard."

Buying a house is commitment. It's roots. It's looking at some place and imagining yourself there for two, three, five, ten years. And for the single woman who wants to imagine herself married, that is a heavy task. In fact, it can be terrifying.

Sabrina tagged onto Jenny's thought: "Girl, I've had the same white walls and pictures leaning up against them since I moved in a year ago. I won't even hang up curtains, but I love interior design. Because if I start decorating, it means I'm planning on being here for a minute. But I don't know what's going to happen. I don't want to commit to that yet."

Waiting plagues us as we make big and small choices. It can come down to furniture, appliances, or decorations. Sometimes we don't think those things are worth the effort for only one person, or sometimes it's exhausting having to be the one to make all the decisions, especially when big money is involved. But we have to do it. We have to do our research. We have to ask our friends. We have to look at our options. Just because we don't have that spouse to affirm or challenge our decisions doesn't mean we're incapable of making them.

We owe it to ourselves to do the things we love, to build lives we enjoy. "You don't have to be married to have a nice home," said Melinda. "You should feel empowered to decorate. To nest. To buy curtains from Target. As a single woman, I spend a lot of time at home, so it needs to be nice."

In the age where *self-care* is a buzzword, I'm willing to

say that this really is a matter of self-care. It's a matter of recognizing your own worth and value and acknowledging that. You deserve nice things. You work hard and shouldn't have to spend your night in a lumpy bed. You fiercely love others and wake up early to work out, and you should do so in clothes that were bought after you graduated high school. You work long hours and then volunteer with refugees, and you should have a bra that's not falling apart.

It's a hard line to build a life that's full and happy while still leaving room for someone else, still operating under the hope that God will fulfill your desire for marriage. For me, this line came down to a single decision: two nightstands or one?

When I was furnishing that apartment in Colorado, I bought my big, fancy bed. I bought a dresser. I bought a cute lamp. Now, do I buy the one nightstand I need, or do I buy two, and pray every night that something other than dust would fill those drawers?

I bought one. This was primarily due to the small square footage of my room, and there have been days when I've been plagued with the fear of getting married and then finding out this line of furniture has been discontinued. It'd be more devastating than when Clinique axed my favorite lip stain.

But it's all a risk, right? Two nightstands and I'm risking the possibility that one will sit unused for two decades before waterbeds come back in style and I decide to upgrade. And right now, I'm risking that if that six-month whirlwind romance I've always planned does come to fruition, we might be left with a lamp sitting on top of a stack of books. And that's okay.

"I'm not going to put my life on hold for someone who may or may not come," said Heather, who has truly shown me the power and grace that radiates from a woman with purpose. "So I kept getting an education, and I excelled in my career, and I've adopted children. Unfortunately, now I feel like people are saying, 'You're too confident,' or 'You don't seem like you want to be married because you're doing all these things.' But this all goes back to the same question: Do we see a single life as an end point—is it a good thing in and of itself?"

We live our single lives, and we give ourselves permission to hope for more. We take the vacations that might have been more fun with someone else, but we snap pictures and try the fried alligator and have a fabulous time regardless. Marriage shouldn't be the gatekeeper to happiness and life experiences.

For some of us, we're not only depriving ourselves of buying something essential or doing something enjoyable, but we're remaining in stagnant, unhealthy environments or relationships, hoping a man or a marriage will fix what's broken.

"One of the hardest parts of being single is knowing what's a healthy relationship with a guy, even if it's not a dating relationship," Melinda said. "For me, women were very safe. It's easy for me to make friends with women. But it's hard to know what a healthy relationship with a male friend looks like or what healthy boundaries are."

Many of us raised in purity culture find ourselves here. We're so scared by the idea of attachment, much less outside of marriage, that we muscle our way through relationships with the opposite sex. When you get married young, you might not realize how few guys you're friends with or how strange those relationships are. But as most of my friends are now married, it's always a funny thing when I find myself watching football with a whole bunch of husbands while the other women are sitting on the patio. I even have to talk myself down from crazy thoughts when one of the menfolk hugs me for longer than a nanosecond or gives me any kind of compliment.

Marriage won't fix these relationships—that's work I need to do. That's my own sticky past that I need to sort through as I establish healthy boundaries and expectations (and remind myself of that healthy sexuality we've already talked about). I know sometimes we subject ourselves to abuse or neglect because we may be limited in our options—and we truly see marriage as an out.

But let me remind us all again of the truth: Your value does not increase in marriage—and right now, you're worth so much more than those kinds of relationships. Someone else choosing to love you won't help you love yourself any more. The Creator of the universe created you in his image, he loves you desperately, and he wants more for you. I want more for you. Marriage won't fix us, because it was never meant to complete us or heal us in the first place.

FIND YOUR JOY

"I don't regret being single," said Courtney in one of our roundtables. "I've become such a great woman in my twenties because I've had to live this single life, and I feel so grateful for this time."

Singleness is hard. This whole book is an ode to how difficult and trying and exhausting and debilitating singleness can be sometimes. But it's also so beautiful. It's filled with growth and service and so much time. My adult single years have been the greatest source of refining I've ever had in my life, and that's after experiencing tremendous personal loss. God is glorified in my unfulfilled longings, and he alone sustains me on those days when it feels easier to hide in my bed than to get out and make decisions and take care of myself. There is good here.

Mary Beth added on to Courtney's thought: "If I had gotten married when I wanted to get married and when I thought I'd be married, I'd be such a different person. I've been able to experience so much growth and healing in the last six years. And six years ago, I wouldn't have been able to be with someone healthy because I wasn't healthy."

"There is joy in singleness," Rachel said. "And I never thought I'd be the girl who said that because I spent all of my twenties wanting to be married. But that didn't happen. And there was a constant grieving because I wasn't married. But then I turned thirty and realized I still had life to live. There's something liberating about surviving your twenties."

There is something liberating. When I choose to look up from what I'm missing to take in all that I have, it's a beautiful sight. I am overwhelmingly blessed. And that doesn't stop me from desiring marriage, and it doesn't stop me from stalking Tim Tebow's social media and imagining *what if?* But it helps—it eases the sting of loneliness and pain and suffering. And some days I even find myself savoring that *joie de vivre*—the "joy of conversation, joy of eating, joy of anything one might do, a comprehensive joy . . . that involves one's whole being."[1]

In Nashville, Emily said something that captures this balancing act: "I struggle with forward thinking. How much do I put into my career? Do I buy this house? It's hard to know what the future holds. I need to have hope for what the Lord may have for me, but I also want to embrace the life that he has given me and live it well."

We misconstrue the gift of singleness as a lifelong thing, as if it's something you have or don't have. If you're single today, you have the gift of singleness. If you're married today, you have the gift of marriage. So today, I have the gift of singleness and all the blessings that come with being single: I have time to pour into people. I have energy and efforts and creativity. I have money, and I don't have to talk with anyone about how I spend my money. If I want the booties, I buy them. *Today* is a gifted season of singleness.

I'm not going to wait for marriage anymore. I'm going to hope for it, I'm going to pray for it, but I'm not going to wait for it. If I truly believe this isn't a season of preparation for something better—that this, that right now, is a life worth living—then I have to make different choices.

One of those choices is to become a mom. Someone once told me that you can always discern the Lord's call on your life based on one question: What is it that, when you imagine your life without it, brings you to tears? For years, I've known the answer to that question wasn't writing or editing or even marriage—it was foster care.

I've lived a hard life. There are lots of miles on these tires, and many of them were on rocky roads. And when I say that I feel led to foster care, it's with full knowledge that apart from salvation, this is the only other calling I've ever felt. My heart beats for children in our broken system, children dreaming of a home.

While the purpose of foster care can, and should, be reunification, I am particularly drawn to the older kids, the ones whose parental rights were terminated months or years ago, and now they're bouncing from foster home to foster home, shelter to group home, until they age out of the system, and they'll be left without a family.

These are my people, my kids. If I could open up a ten-bedroom ranch and bring them in today, I would. I want to give them a home, a chance to succeed in this world, and a place to fall when they fail. I want to show them that just because you're twelve years old, and you have been through unspeakable pain and trauma, you are not beyond loving— you are not beyond redemption.

I was ten when the Lord started bringing people into my life. Aunts and uncles, mentors and teachers, parents of friends. They each adopted me into their families. They paid for my meals. They hugged me extra tight. I was raised by a village who saw that, in spite of my lashing out and my propensity toward lying and my neediness, I wasn't irredeemable. I can't even imagine where I'd be without all of those people who weren't required to love me but chose to anyway.

As God molds my heart and paves the way for me to pursue foster care, I know it's a risk. It would be so much easier with a husband, and that's how I've always imagined it. We'd feel called to this together, and we'd invest time and energy in loving those who need it most. But, at least so far, that vision hasn't come to pass, so I must be faithful to my calling even as I walk this path on my own. Being a single mom isn't easy—it requires tremendous sacrifice and juggling and help. It's not a path I ever thought I'd willingly choose. But in October 2015, when I was telling a dear friend (then stranger), Belinda Bauman, that I couldn't wait to be married so I could do foster care, her response was one that's now carved on my heart: "But why do you have to wait for marriage?"

I don't. And neither do you.

CONCLUSION

Helping Singles Find a Place in the Church

"We should be neither overly elated about being married nor overly disappointed by not being so—because Christ is the only spouse that can truly fulfill us and God's family the only family that will truly embrace and satisfy us."[1]

So, if you're not single, if you've just been eavesdropping on the single ladies' conversation for the past two hundred pages, I have no idea what you might be feeling. It might be confusion, because you were married young or at an age where you never experienced many of the struggles or frustrations I'm describing. Perhaps you're feeling angry on our behalf (good!). Or maybe you're defensive, because when you hear a whole bunch of people come together to criticize the thing you love, it can be painful.

I didn't want to end this book without giving the church a few quick notes. These aren't groundbreaking, and if you sit down with any group of single people, you'll probably hear many of them rattled off in the first few minutes. These are simply ways we can better bring singles into the body of Christ—because the local churches that don't work hard to incorporate singles into their infrastructure are ones that won't be around in fifty years.

For starters, our language has to change. If there's anything I want this book to emphasize, it's that the words we use and the phrases we spout, even out of love, can be damaging and demoralizing.

When the majority of my conversations with married women in my church revolve around my love life (or lack thereof), that's only working to remind me that without marriage, I have little to offer. Instead of leading with "Oh, are you seeing anyone?" I'd love to be engaged in conversation by being asked, "What are you doing for the kingdom? What are you passionate about? Why do you talk about foster care so much?" Those are the kinds of questions that reinforce my worth and contributions right now, not the role of wife and mother I could potentially adopt.

With our language, may we be vigilant in fighting against our tendency to portray the family as providing what only God can—fulfillment, security, joy, hope, purpose, and significance. Motherhood is not the greatest joy, singleness is not best spent in preparing for marriage, and I won't find peace and security in a husband.

In addition to careful language, intentional representation matters. The Christian community has buzzed in the last few years with the importance of encouraging diversity in thought, ethnicity, even age. But I'd love to see more single representation in the church. When we only see married people serving in leadership positions, offering Communion, or opening the service in prayer, that's a problem. That's sending a message to me, a single woman, that I am not ready, fit, or able to serve.

Pastors who are single should not be penalized. Single female missionaries shouldn't be the hardest group to fund. Single people should be sought out for committees, panels, and service opportunities in the church—not because they have more time to serve but because their input is invaluable and could not be gained elsewhere. As Liz said in one of our roundtables, "I don't know that I've ever been to a Sunday school or small group meant for single people that's actually led and planned by a single person. Let's elevate singles into positions of leadership, and not assume that there's a selfishness or fatal flaw in them."

While we're overhauling the church, let's also completely revamp singles ministries. Those two words can make my skin crawl. In most minds, singles ministries are more of a deterrent rather than an incentive. I've heard this ministry used synonymously with "meat market" or "singles buffet." I'd like fried okra with a side of seminary grad student, please.

And most of the time, as Liz noted, events hosted by singles ministries often exist to marry off the one awkward thirty-seven-year-old man church members try foisting upon all the women who accidently wander in. I'd rather take my chances and meet a guy in a restaurant or online rather than roll the dice with a singles ministry that may make us link arms and scramble together as we try and untie the human knot.

Yet I'm still encouraged, because all these things—language, leadership, programming—they're all fixable. We can, and should, make space for singles in the church. This isn't a pipe dream—it's a plan for fostering more growth and community by meeting the needs of those who've been marginalized by the church's crusade for marriage. We must examine our hearts, cast out the idols, and look to Christ alone. He is our only hope.

ACKNOWLEDGMENTS

Okay, if you've just finished this after a midnight marathon reading session or you're on the subway on your way home from work, and you've been faithfully coming back to this book every day on your commute until you were done: *Yay! We made it! Thank you!*

Now I have to give a shout-out to all the important people who helped breathe life into this thing. It should be a pile of pages in a box on my closet floor, but it's not, and that's a miracle.

So, first, because it's literally a miracle, let's give God a handclap of praise. Or a high five. Or maybe just an audible *hallelujah* wherever you are. The fact that this book exists is equivalent to the parting of the Red Sea or the exorcism of the demons into those pigs.

And then a huge thank-you to Nelson Books, who have been nothing short of wonderful. Being chosen by them was like Johnny asking Baby to dance in *Dirty Dancing*. All I brought to this party was a watermelon, but apparently, that was enough. I'm so glad they brought me in, shaped me up, gave me this beautiful cover, and presented me to the world like a sixteen-year-old debutante at her coming-out party.

The gold medal should go to my editor, Jessica, who sculpted this pile of words into a much prettier pile of words. You're a master at what you do, and I'm so grateful you chose me (and I chose you!). Can we be friends now?

To Blair and Don: Somehow "oh, my *agent* . . ." comes up in conversation far more often than you ever realized it would. So thankful I have D. C. Jacobson to shamelessly name-drop.

To my mom and dad and Cooper and Marie, but mainly my two-year-old niece, Abby: So many times when I pick my battles, it's with you in mind. I hope the world is kind to you. Auntie loves you!

One quick shout-out to my best friends, my cheer-leaders who have spurred me on through this whole process. You're all over the country, but you're unfailingly support-ive. You're the best. Also, you're all wearing ugly taffeta dresses for the wedding—I'm thinking lemon meringue.

Around 80 percent of the time, writing is a solitary ven-ture. But 20 percent of the time, writing is filled with people who buy into your vision, your plan for this book, and they come alongside you. For a book like this, a book anchored on the concept of roundtables, I needed people to buy in. And they did, over and over again.

I am indebted to all of the women who came and partic-ipated in the roundtables in Chicago, Nashville, Lynchburg, and Colorado Springs. I'm so grateful for the women who did smaller group discussions and one-on-one interviews with me. The way you ladies were able to be honest and vulnerable so I could share your stories in this book is one of the bravest things I've ever seen. Thank you.

Thanks to all the people who read this sucker and offered feedback when it was still underperforming and overflowing with adverbs: Amanda, Tory, Allison, Ian, Liz, Morgan, and Jenna. Because of you, I am less unintentionally offensive and intentionally repetitive.

For CAPC, who taught me that while writing the book was a solitary venture, publishing it didn't have to be. I have never felt alone in this, and it's because of y'all. You're family, and I love you.

This list would be incomplete without acknowledging all of the men who asked me out only to provide truly awful company, stood me up for our 10:00 a.m. brunch plans, cried in the middle of our date, led me on for several years, and mercilessly broke my heart—a few times: None of you are likely going to read this book, but thanks for all the great material. If it becomes a bestseller, I'll send you each a fruitcake.

And to you! My precious, sweet new friends. I want you each to find me and follow me and e-mail me and tell me all your thoughts, because more than anything this book is a conversation, and I'm dying for you to join in. (What am I missing? What are your struggles? How can we help one another more?) Thank you for sticking with me. I'm so lucky to have you, and let's all be best friends forever. Who's in for a bulk order of those plastic BFF heart necklaces?

ABOUT THE AUTHOR

After accidentally kissing dating goodbye, Joy Beth Smith has spent much of her adult life flying solo. In the meantime, she works at *Christianity Today* as a managing editor and people-watches at the gym while listening to audiobooks. JB loves eavesdropping, gas-station hot dogs, and uncomfortable discussions about sexuality. At a time when people in the church are desperate for authentic, vulnerable conversation, who better to start the dialogue than one of their own—a single girl from the South with two carry-ons of neatly folded emotional baggage?

NOTES

Chapter 1: God Doesn't Owe You a Husband

1. Paige Benton Brown, "Singled Out for Good," Reformed Youth Ministries, October 10, 2014, https://rymonline.org/resources/posts/singled-out-for-good-1.
2. Matthew 16:22–23.

Chapter 4: Jesus Might Not Meet All Your Needs

1. Oswald Chambers, *My Utmost for His Highest* (Uhrichsville, OH: Barbour, 2000), January 7.
2. Chris Tomlin, "In the Secret," Metrolyrics, http://www.metrolyrics.com/in-the-secret-lyrics-chris-tomlin.html.
3. David Crowder Band, "No One Like You," Metrolyrics, http://www.metrolyrics.com/no-one-like-you-lyrics-david-crowder.html.
4. Matt Maher, "Lord I Need You," Metrolyrics, http://www.metrolyrics.com/lord-i-need-you-lyrics-matt-maher.html.
5. Lifehouse, "Hanging by a Moment," Metrolyrics, http://www.metrolyrics.com/hanging-by-a-moment-lyrics-lifehouse.html.
6. Penny March, "I Will Follow Him," Metrolyrics, http://www.metrolyrics.com/i-will-follow-him-lyrics-sister-act.html.
7. Proverbs 27:17.

8. Timothy Keller, *The Meaning of Marriage* (New York: Penguin, 2011), 95.

Chapter 5: Sorry, God Might Not Give You Your Heart's Desires

1. Matthew Henry, *Zondervan* NIV *Matthew Henry Commentary* (Grand Rapids: Zondervan, 1992).
2. Thomas Umstattd Jr., "The Courtship Prosperity Gospel," *Thomas Umstattd Jr.* (blog), August 20, 2015, http://www .thomasumstattd.com/2015/08/courtship-prosperity-gospel/.
3. John Piper, Twitter post, March 1, 2016, 5:04 a.m., https:// twitter.com/johnpiper/status/704653441533132800?lang=en.

Chapter 6: What Is Sexuality?

1. Kim Gaines Eckert, *Things Your Mother Never Told You: A Woman's Guide to Sexuality* (Downers Grove, IL: IVP, 2014).
2. Ibid., 24.
3. Debra Hirsch, *Redeeming Sex: Naked Conversations About Sexuality and Spirituality* (Downers Grove, IL: IVP, 2015), 26.
4. Dan Allender and Tremper Longman III, *God Loves Sex: An Honest Conversation About Sexual Desire and Holiness* (Grand Rapids, MI: Baker Books, 2014), xi.
5. Catherine Buni, "The Case for Teaching Kids 'Vagina,' 'Penis,' and Vulva,'" *Atlantic,* April 15, 2013, https://www .theatlantic.com/health/archive/2013/04/the-case-for-teaching -kids-vagina-penis-and-vulva/274969/.
6. J. K. Rowling, *Harry Potter and the Sorcerer's Stone* (New York: Scholastic, 1995), 298.
7. Hirsch, *Redeeming Sex*, 26.
8. Ibid., 49.
9. Jim Cotter, *Pleasure, Pain and Passion: Some Perspective on Sexuality and Spirituality* (Sheffield, UK: Cairns, 1988), 71.

Chapter 7: Masturbation, Porn, and Other Big-Ticket Items

1. Allender and Longman, *God Loves Sex*, 42–43.
2. C. S. Lewis, *Yours, Jack* (Grand Rapids: Zondervan, 2008), 292–93.
3. Allender and Longman, *God Loves Sex*, 140.
4. Rachel Held Evans, "Christians and Masturbation: Seven Perspectives," *RachelHeldEvans.com* (blog), June 3, 2013, https://rachelheldevans.com/blog/christians-masturbation.
5. Ibid.
6. James Dobson, *Preparing for Adolescence* (Grand Rapids: Revell, 2005), 69.
7. James Dobson, "Dr. Dobson's Initial Letter Regarding Masturbation," Overcoming Lust, http://www.overcoming -lust.com/httpwww-overcoming-lust-comdr-james-dobsons -open-letter-masturbation/.
8. Wesley Hill, "Escaping the Prison of the Self," *First Things* (blog), February 10, 2014, https://www.firstthings.com/blogs /firstthoughts/2014/02/escaping-the-prison-of-the-self.
9. Held Evans, "Christians and Masturbation."
10. Covenant Eyes, "Pornography Statistics: 2015," Covenanteyes.com, http://www.covenanteyes.com/pornstats/.
11. Dave Kinnaman, "The Porn Phenomenon," Barna.com, 2016, https://www.barna.com/the-porn-phenomenon/.
12. Ibid.

Chapter 8: Sexuality Isn't a Science

1. 1 Corinthians 6:18–20, 7:2; 1 Thessalonians 4:3–5; Galatians 5:1–20.
2. Brené Brown, "Listening to Shame," lecture, TED2012 Conference, video, 20:38, filmed March 2012, https://www .ted.com/talks/brene_brown_listening_to_shame.
3. Edward T. Welch, *Shame Interrupted: How God Lifts the*

Pain of Worthlessness and Rejection (Greensboro, NC: New Growth Press, 2012), 2.

4. Brown, "Listening to Shame."

5. Curt Thompson, *The Soul of Shame: Retelling the Stories We Believe About Ourselves* (Downers Grove, IL: IVP, 2015), 126–27.

6. Ibid., 35.

7. Eckert, *Things Your Mother Never Told You*, 14–15.

8. Nehemiah 3:28.

Chapter 10: Dating Is a Cesspool, and Other Lessons

1. Kathleen Elkins, "Warren Buffett and Sheryl Sandberg Agree on the Most Important Decision You Will Make," CNBC, http://www.cnbc.com/2017/02/07/warren-buffett-and-sheryl -sandberg-agree-on-most-important-decision.html.

Chapter 12: Don't Spend Your Singleness Preparing for Marriage

1. Timothy Keller, *The Meaning of Marriage* (New York: Penguin, 2011), 28.

2. Ibid., 132.

3. C. S. Lewis, "The Weight of Glory," Verber, http://www.verber .com/mark/xian/weight-of-glory.pdf.

4. Matthew 6:33.

Chapter 13: Don't Wait for Marriage

1. Warren Shibles, *Humor Reference Guide: A Comprehensive Classification and Analysis* (Carbondale, IL: Southern Illinois University Press, 1997), 187.

Conclusion

1. Timothy Keller, *The Meaning of Marriage* (New York: Penguin, 2011), 198.